T0121373

"From the messy and chaotic world of substance misuse (in which we drug and alcohol professionals work) too few stories of hope emerge. Here is an intensely personal and painful memoir—a story of tragedy and triumph, begging to be heard. In her unpretentious yet immensely readable style, the author shares her journey and points to the *source* of all personal freedom. This story continues to *inspire* me and I know will do the same for countless others!"

David Entermann
Alcohol and Other Drugs Clinical Worker

"For several years my husband and I lived in certain rehabilitation centres in Central Asia, teaching English to students. We saw firsthand, the devastation caused by substance abuse. In her book, the author takes us on a raw journey through her years as a drug addict; we are then given the privilege of walking with her out of those horrific years in to the wonder and joy of a *new* life! Her story will reach in to the hearts of many and will inspire others to pursue the path to freedom."

Janice Mau
Author of *Samovars & Shashlik: Gems of an Overseas Adventure*

For This Cause

Against All Odds

Nascosta InCristo

BALBOA.
PRESS
A DIVISION OF HAY HOUSE

Copyright © 2015 Nascosta InCristo.

All rights reserved. No part of this book may be used or reproduced by any means, graphic, electronic, or mechanical, including photocopying, recording, taping or by any information storage retrieval system without the written permission of the author except in the case of brief quotations embodied in critical articles and reviews.

Balboa Press books may be ordered through booksellers or by contacting:

Balboa Press
A Division of Hay House
1663 Liberty Drive
Bloomington, IN 47403
www.balboapress.com.au
1 (877) 407-4847

Because of the dynamic nature of the Internet, any web addresses or links contained in this book may have changed since publication and may no longer be valid. The views expressed in this work are solely those of the author and do not necessarily reflect the views of the publisher, and the publisher hereby disclaims any responsibility for them.

The author of this book does not dispense medical advice or prescribe the use of any technique as a form of treatment for physical, emotional, or medical problems without the advice of a physician, either directly or indirectly. The intent of the author is only to offer information of a general nature to help you in your quest for emotional and spiritual well-being. In the event you use any of the information in this book for yourself, which is your constitutional right, the author and the publisher assume no responsibility for your actions.

Any people depicted in stock imagery provided by Thinkstock are models, and such images are being used for illustrative purposes only. Certain stock imagery © Thinkstock.

Scripture from the New King James Version (NKJV). Copyright 1982 by Thomas Nelson. Used by permission. All rights reserved. Scriptures from the Holy Bible, New International Version (NIV) copyright 1973, 1978, 1984, 2011 by Biblica, Inc. Used with permission. All rights reserved worldwide. Information was taken from an article in the eleventh edition of YOOZ magazine produced by WASUA (West Australian Substance Users Association) with their permission. The poem "The Church of the Lord Jesus Christ" is included in this manuscript with the kind permission of the author, Robert Fergusson.

Print information available on the last page.

ISBN: 978-1-4525-2814-4 (sc)
ISBN: 978-1-4525-2815-1 (e)

Balboa Press rev. date: 03/25/2015

For you, Jesus.

Pilate therefore said to Him, "Are You a king then?" Jesus answered, "You say rightly that I am a king. For this cause I was born, and for this cause I have come into the world, that I should bear witness to the truth. Everyone who is of the truth hears my voice."

—John 18:37 (New King James Version)

GLOSSARY

Bikies—members of a gang of motorbikers
Block—ounce of heroin
Coo-ees—slang term for friends/mates
Coota—West Australian street slang for pure, high-grade speed
Crack—cocaine
Cone—dried marijuana smoked in a joint or a bong
Duchy Pone—street slang for cone
Eight-ball—eighth of an ounce of a powdered drug (usually cocaine)
Fit—syringe, pick
Gear—intravenous (IV) drugs
Goee—West Australian slang for Speed
Grey Nurse— street name for a 100mg morphine tablet
Gunja, ganya, ganja—Indigenous terms for marijuana
Hanging out—withdrawing from drugs/alcohol
Home bake—turn morphine into heroin
Home bake, smack, harry—slang terms for heroin
In the sticks—away from town/out in the bush/country areas
Marijuana—weed, bud
Morph—morphine
My Shout—my turn to pay/treat someone by paying for them
Nod, nodded off, smashed—sedated/high/wiped out
Pick—syringe
Pot—drugs, usually marijuana
Session—smoking dope
Shot—fix, taste, injection of drugs

Six pack—a set of six bottles/cans of alcohol
Smashed on cones—high on marijuana
Speed, whiz, goee, rev—amphetamines
Streetie—slang term for street kid/someone who lives on the streets
Toke—puff on a joint
Wag—skip school

CONTENTS

FOREWORD

I have read this book with deep emotion in my heart and tears in my eyes. This is not a piece of fanciful fiction or theoretical theology. This is real and this is raw.

This is a journey of heroic faith from the depth of human depravity and brokenness to a place of hope, healing, and confidence. That journey is not yet finished, but the view from this point gives reason to celebrate and an assurance of a great future.

I remember the first day I met the author, nine years ago. It was a cold winter's day. She was sitting on the step outside the place where we held church services. She was huddled in a ball trying to catch the sun and get warm. Tears were running down her cheeks.

"Do you think God can love me?" she whispered.

"Yes, He can and He does!" I replied with compassion and conviction. In hindsight, I am humbled to realize I had little idea of the immensity of that truth and the power of God to redeem and transform a life. I am filled with awe.

Anyone who reads this book with an open mind and open heart will be encouraged and instructed. If you are desperate, there is hope; if you are addicted, there is a way to freedom. If you are a pastor, have absolute confidence in the power of the God you represent, and if you are a theological pundit, forget your foolish arguments about cheap grace because grace is more costly and effective than you can ever understand.

My wife and I count it a great privilege to have been part of the author's story over these last nine years. We honour the families of the local church who have embraced her and her family with love, acceptance, and generosity. It takes a community of people, not just a couple of individuals, to nurture wholeness and healing. The local church is still the hope of the world!

I commend this book to you wholeheartedly. It will do you good.

Pastor R. Hill
12th December 2012

NOTE FROM THE AUTHOR

Some believe drug addicts cannot break free and live whole, healthy lives. This book is my personal testimony declaring, "Yes, we can!" It is also a tribute to the awesome power of God.

My book is an honest account of my life as I remember it. I have not tried to soften events or hide the reality of the way I lived. I was a drug addict and lived a criminal lifestyle. God pursued me through those painful years, revealing that He truly does love the sinning soul and wants to bring healing and wholeness to all who reach out to Him.

I pray that my story will bring hope to others struggling with addiction. I pray it will also be a warning.

I do not hold any of my family members responsible for the destructive lifestyle I fell in to. The choices I made were mine, and I have suffered the consequences of those choices. For the sorrow and pain I brought to their lives, I can only ask forgiveness. My deepest apologies to my children who went through so much. I thank God that those days are long gone and I am now able to be the mother God called me to be.

I owe my life to God, so it is with joy and pride in Him that I bring you my story.

God bless and be with you.

—*Nassa*

INTRODUCTION

It was late and too cold to go outside, but the pregnant couple wanted to go home to their own bed rather than stay overnight. I offered to lend them my second car.

"Just bring it back sometime tomorrow," I said, handing over the keys.

Days later there was no sign of the car and no word from the couple. They were not replying to our messages or answering any of our calls. My partner and I decided to visit them, taking a spare car key with us.

We knocked on the door of their house for some time, but nobody answered, so we figured no one was home. Our car was parked in the driveway, so we decided we might as well take it.

To our shock, as we began to reverse down the driveway, the woman's husband flew out the front door with a tomahawk in his hand—a tomahawk that he hurled at the car, smashing the front windscreen.

Some days later I was driving around delivering drug deals (despite the broken windscreen) when I heard my phone ringing over the sound of the music playing. It was my partner. He was begging me to bring the car back because some bikies had him at knifepoint in our home. They were threatening to hurt him if I did not immediately return the car.

Someone took the phone from my partner, and a deep voice rumbled at me. "Hey, love! It's a coffin-cheater here! How about you bring back that car and everything will be okay."

"What the f*ck! That's *my* car, mate!" I said crossly. "There's only one coffin-cheater that I know of, and His name is *Jesus*! (Bwahahaha!)"

Beep ... beep ... beep went the phone.

CHAPTER ONE

Chores and Holy Communion

Not once did I ever see my father loving my mother, or vice versa. They were always arguing. It was as though they hated each other, and as a child, I often wondered why.

Mum and Dad both worked hard to make ends meet. When one came home from work, the other left for work.

I remember an elderly friend of the family looking after me when I was five years old. She was a sweet old woman, but she had the habit of kissing me repeatedly on the cheek. That was okay, but some days she would have white foam in the corners of her lips, which would scare the living daylights out of me. I began to dread staying with her. I would hide in her wardrobe while she went up and down the street crying out my name in Italian and repeatedly calling, *"Dove stai?"* ("Where are you?") I was petrified she would find me and kiss me again.

My parents were born in Italy and met in Australia in 1970. I am not too sure of how it all went, as I have only heard one side of the story. Mum would often share details with me, but Dad never spoke about it, period. He would shy away from questions by making light of them. It was always that way with Dad. A primary example is a time when he was building something out of wood. Dad loved to make things, and to me, this thing looked like a paddleboat.

"What are you making, Dad?" I asked.

"A boat," he replied. (Dad loved to go fishing.)

As I was admiring his handiwork, I noticed a hole about four inches wide at one end. Concerned for Dad's safety, I said, "Dad, it can't be a boat. There's a hole in it." Dad just laughed and went about his work. Several weeks later, I learned the "boat" was actually a wine press!

I was born in December 1971. I am the oldest of three girls, with a four-year gap between each of us. I remember Mum telling me that her waters broke four days prior to my birth. I believe my personal fight for life began from that point on. Birth without water would have been a painful experience for both parties, and Mum still likes to remind me of it.

When I was three years old, my parents went back to Italy for a while but then returned to the West Coast of Australia in time for me to start school.

School was extremely difficult. I was five or six years old and could not speak a word of English. The kids in grade one would make fun of me because a foreign language was coming out of my mouth. They would laugh and tease me by mimicking what I had said in Italian. Mum told me one day that the teachers were not sure what to do with me, as they could not cater to my lack of English. I fell behind in my studies, finding it extremely difficult to learn—so much so that the school placed me in special-education classes for all of my subjects.

When I was eight years old we were living in a little town where Mum and Dad ran a pizza bar, the only one in that area. They were so busy that I had to help them at home and in the business. My childhood went out the window. I was left at home by myself to look after my two sisters, the youngest being only eight months old. I have to admit it was very scary, but someone had to do it and the task fell to me.

Mum and Dad—mainly my mother—were very strict Roman Catholics: "Father, Son, and Holy Spirit." However, it did not feel as if there was anything of the Father, the Son, or the Holy Spirit in our household. If there had been, they must have left with the first swear words spoken by my dear mum. Every second word was f*ck this or bastard that, and because she had an accent, it sounded funny.

Every Sunday, Mum would wake me up to go to church. No one else went; it was just me. I would walk to church and back every Sunday. It was through the Catholic faith that I received my Holy Communion sacrament. This meant I was able to have "communion with Christ" by receiving the bread and wine, which represented the Last Supper Jesus had with his disciples before he was crucified. The cracker or bread (or host) represented the body of Christ, and the wine or grape juice represented the blood of Christ. This was all very important to the Roman Catholic religion, and I had to do it, no questions asked. Without my sacrament of Holy Communion, I could not partake in the communion.

Four years later Mum and Dad decided to sell the pizza bar and move closer to the city. I was turning twelve, and their decision devastated me. The thought of leaving my school and my friends distressed me deeply. I recall Dad yelling at me to get in the car on that final day as we were leaving. I simply did not want to go.

Once we arrived in the city area, we stayed with some friends until Dad found a house to buy. Dad bought an ice cream business, which I admit was great fun. Mum found work in a restaurant.

My home life was not what you would call peaceful. Mum and Dad would often get verbally abusive toward each other over money issues. With both of them working all the time, I was again the one who ended up doing most of the chores around the house: cleaning, cooking, and looking after my sisters. I just wanted to be a kid and do what kids do, but there was no room or time in my life for that. As much as I hated it, I had to continue helping.

My parents were very strict, and this meant no going out with friends or attending sleepovers. Even riding my bike on our street was an issue. By this stage, home no longer felt like a home. It felt more like a prison. School became a place of escape and freedom.

As I approached age thirteen, I expected a little more liberty. As I saw it, if I was old enough to cook, clean, and babysit, I should be old enough to hang out with friends. But that was not how things happened. While friends were experiencing the joys of freedom and doing the fun stuff kids do, I was stuck at home. This angered me so much I would lock myself in my room and dance away my frustrations to popular song tracks before settling down with my journal to write about how much my life sucked.

Every day I would return home from school to find the inevitable housework waiting for me—housework that had to be done before Mum got home. The fact that I had a large amount of homework to complete before the next day made no difference. Those chores were the priority!

On one occasion, after finishing all the chores, I noticed a little bit of pasta sauce had stuck to the bottom of a pot. It was not that much, so I did not worry about it. I always took pride in my efforts, hoping Mum would appreciate the things I did, and on this occasion I was still hoping she would show appreciation. Instead, when she returned home, she focused on that little bit of stuck pasta sauce, criticizing me for it. I did not hear one word of thanks for the work I had done. I felt it was very unfair. She did not seem to appreciate my efforts at all—efforts that I thought were pretty good, considering my young age.

I do not remember receiving expressions of thanks or praise or ever getting a pat on the back. As a result, I became very discouraged. I grew tired of my parents never acknowledging my efforts or me. I was also tired of them not acknowledging anything that interested me personally. Take, for example, dancing! I loved to dance. I remember doing a fair bit of it at school. When I asked Mum and Dad if I could join a dance school, they sent me off to marching school instead. Dad thought a little "army discipline" would not go astray. This made me so angry. Neither of my parents was listening to me at all. I had had enough!

Rebellion took a deep hold in my heart.

In the summer of 1984 I started high school. High school was a huge deal compared to primary school, and you could easily feel lost. I remember feeling very lonely, as there was only a handful of kids from my primary school and I did not really know them that well. Every recess and lunch break, the girls' toilets were crammed with boys and girls smoking cigarettes. I would slip into the first cubical, do my business, and quickly run out again. I was frightened of those other kids but at the same time intrigued by their bold behaviour. It looked like they didn't have a care in the world and were very at ease with themselves. For my own part, I always felt tormented and stressed out.

One afternoon, while walking home from school, I caught up with a girl who walked the same route as me. I was nervous around her at first, but she introduced herself and was friendly. Her name was Cayse. She held out an open packet of cigarettes, offering me one. I will never forget it.

"Sure. I could really do with one of these," I said to her. (This was not my first smoke. When I was eleven, I would steal Mum's cigarettes before she gave them up.)

We both smoked as we walked and talked, and I shared my inner frustrations with her. She in turn shared how her life was generally very easygoing.

I learnt that her parents were much older than mine. Cayse also informed me that her dad was dying of cancer.

When we got to her house, which was at the top of my street, Cayse invited me in for a cold cordial drink and introduced me to her family. They seemed very nice. I envied how peaceful and easygoing her life appeared compared to mine.

In one of my special-ed English classes, I developed a huge crush on one of the boys. His name was Bejay. He was tall, thin, blond, blue-eyed, and not afraid to break the rules. I liked this about him. Maybe because of the rebellion in my own heart, certain types of people drew me—people who inspired in me a sense of power over my situation at home.

One Monday morning, two boys waltzed into the special-ed English class late, both of them smelling of cigarettes. They walked by my desk and sat down in their seats behind me. They were laughing and whispering. After a while their behaviour began to distract me, and before I knew it I was laughing with them, which resulted in all three of us being given detention and scab duty (picking up rubbish) at lunchtime.

One day in the middle of maths class, I overheard the same two boys talking about a disco. Every month, the community held a disco in the recreation hall of the footy oval (football training ground and games area), which was located at the end of our street. I wanted to go because Bejay was going to be there, but I did not know how I would do it. (My parents would not even let me ride my bike up and down our street!) I started pestering Mum. I had a whole month to convince her, and I was confident that if I nagged her enough, she would give in—which she eventually did—only because it was a stone's throw away from our home and Mum thought she would be able to keep her eye on me.

At the age of fourteen I was still very naïve, so when I got to the footy oval, I was staggered to see it crawling with kids all smoking and drinking alcohol. I walked into the disco and found only a handful of kids dancing, none of whom I knew—and no sign of Bejay.

I went outside to see who I could find. As I walked toward a streetlight at the edge of the park, I heard a voice call out my name. My heart skipped a beat when I saw it was Bejay. He was drunk, sprawled out on the grass. I helped him to his feet, all the while enjoying the fact that he had his arms around and all over me.

Taking me by the hand, Bejay led me into the dark oval where he introduced me to his friends, who were drinking near a block of toilets. He then handed me a can of beer, which I opened and drank before realizing time had gotten away from me. It was way past my curfew.

I quickly ran home to find my mum waiting for me with a fly swatter. She beat me with it, all the while yelling, "Never again!"

She meant it. I had just cut my rope of freedom down to a shoelace, and the only freedom I was ever going to experience was the trampoline in my backyard!

The following day at school, I found Bejay in the canteen area scabbing money from other students. He even asked me for fifty cents, but when I told him I did not have it, he walked away to continue scabbing off others.

The next morning I woke up early so I could sneak into my dad's ice cream van to steal his loose change. I took five dollars' worth of fifty-cent pieces. Bejay was my primary reason for doing it. I knew in my heart that I was buying his friendship but I did not care. I liked Bejay heaps, and at the time, I felt he made my life worth living. I was prepared to do anything to get his attention, even if it was at my dad's expense. I did this every day, knowing that while I had money, Bejay would hang around.

One morning near the school canteen, Bejay asked if I wanted to go have a cigarette.

"Where will we go?" I asked him.

He pointed to a house across the street and opposite the school. "C'mon! There's a girl there I want you to meet."

Jade, one of the popular girls, lived there. Many kids used to wag (skip) school, going over to her house to hang out. It explained why this girl was hardly ever at school.

Until this point I had never broken any school rules, and I found the prospect scary yet exciting at the same time. Bejay and I looked around, hoping none of the teachers on duty would see us. He led the way, and we ran quickly through the front door of the school, making it to the house without any problems.

I could not believe how many kids were at this girl's house, all of them wagging school. They were in the backyard smoking cigarettes and laughing at Jade who was supposedly drunk and doing dolphin dives in her aboveground swimming pool. It was quite funny, but since I was the new kid on the block, I was not game to laugh openly. Eventually she stopped swimming. Then she spotted me standing in the crowd and stared right at me.

Bejay introduced us. Jade was unbelievably gorgeous. Her green eyes and blonde hair said it all. She really was stunning. Her fun-loving free spirit made a real impression on me.

Over time, the footy oval became our local hangout, and my new friends became my priority. I felt loved and respected—the opposite of what I felt at home—when I was with my friends at the oval. It was there that I had my first toke of marijuana. I rolled around on the grass laughing uncontrollably after smoking it.

Every Friday night I would take off from home and not return until Sunday night. I copped many floggings from my parents but I did not care; it was worth the freedom. Finally, my father kicked me out of the house after I stole and damaged his car. He'd had enough of my delinquency, and I was forced to pack my bags and leave the family home. I did not know where to go, so I decided to walk to my new friend Jade's place. After I told her what had happened, she begged her mum to let me stay with them.

One Friday night, when Jade and I did not come home, her mum's patience ran out. In a fit of anger she demanded I leave. I do not blame her, as I would have done the same if I had been in her position. Unfortunately, it meant I was now homeless. I began to stay here, there, and everywhere, waking up some mornings in strange places, such as telecommunication buildings or large water pipes that lay around in parks.

Early one morning, after a party in another suburb with a gang of Italian boys, I staggered across the road to a house belonging to friends of the family. I crashed out on the lounge, which was on their veranda. Our families had known each other for years. A few hours later, the eldest of the two boys in the family woke me up. (He was a gang member.) Surprised to find me there, he asked what I was doing. I told him Mum and Dad had kicked me out and I had no place to go. He told his mum, who let me stay that night in their granny flat.

The next morning, a tall police officer woke me up. "Wake up, Sleeping Beauty. Get dressed; we're going to court!"

Being half-asleep and still drunk, I managed to ask, "What for?"

"Your mum says you're uncontrollable—she can't control you anymore."

Rubbing my eyes, I got up. Once I was dressed, I staggered out to the police car. After arriving at the court, the cops locked me up in a holding cell, telling me to wait until it was my turn to face the magistrate. In the same cell were some girls who were in on burglary charges. I had never been in a holding cell before, and I felt overwhelmed by what was happening.

That afternoon, the court declared me a ward of the state. This meant my parents were no longer responsible for me and the government was. After court finished, I was taken to a high-security hostel, where I had to stay until they could find suitable foster care for me.

I was furious! I could not believe my parents had given up on me so quickly and easily. I was so angry, it felt like I had a furnace raging inside. I remember thinking there were going to be major repercussions. I could not see any good coming out of my parents' decision. Not knowing what lay ahead for me, I felt deeply insecure and very much alone.

CHAPTER TWO

I Am with You Always!

When I arrived at the hostel, one of the workers showed me to my room. I was the only kid there at the time, but the worker informed me that kids would be coming in and out at all hours of the day and night. I dropped my bag on the floor and sat on the cold, hard bed. I felt very scared and lonely as I stared at the steel-barred windows.

As a child, I would often pray, having conversations with God. As I sat there, I began to seek comfort from Him. As I prayed, I heard a quiet voice within me saying, *It's okay. Everything is going to be all right.* At the same time, I felt myself embraced by warmth, as if God was giving me a great big hug. Peace filled me, and I did not feel as scared or alone anymore. This was my first real encounter with God. From that day on, I believed He was close by, watching over me.

So there I was in the high-security hostel waiting for foster care. Two weeks went by. Nothing happened, nobody came—it was not happening for me. They moved me to another children's hostel, which was just up the road. This place was great compared to the first one. Firstly, there were no bars on the windows, and secondly, there were four other kids living there. Things were more flexible with a ten thirty curfew on the weekend and nine during the week. We were free to go out, provided we were home by curfew.

A week later on a Friday afternoon, Baz, one of the boys in the hostel, told me he was meeting up with some friends in the city and asked if I would like to go with him. It sounded like fun so I smiled and agreed to go.

He bought some beers from the local drive-through bottle shop, and we drank as we walked to the city. By the time we got there, I was feeling a little drunk. We walked down one of the main malls until we saw three of his friends, two boys and a girl.

"Hey!" Baz yelled. He introduced us. "This is Colt, Jake, and Moxie. Guys, meet Angel!" (Angel was my nickname.)

"Hi," I said.

"What's happening?" Baz asked.

Jake replied, "We're going for a drink. Want to come?"

"Yeah, we'll come!" Baz said, looking back at me for confirmation.

Jake and his mates led the way through the streets of the city until we came to a beer and wine shop. They bought a carton of beer and suggested we go to some council gardens to drink it. In a nice secluded spot, we drank and had a good time getting to know each other. When I asked them where they lived, they said they were homeless street kids, unable to live at home with family for many different reasons. (I remember thinking that explained why they looked a little rough around the edges.)

I was feeling pretty drunk when the town clock suddenly gonged ten times. With only half an hour left to curfew, Baz suggested we cab it home fast as he did not want to get into trouble. We said good-bye and ran quickly to the taxi stand. I could have quite easily stayed behind with the street kids, as I was curious to know where they were going to sleep that night. As far as I was concerned, I was just like those street kids—not belonging to anyone in particular.

As the taxi drove us back to the hostel, I remembered the times when I had visualized what street kids looked like. After Jade's mum kicked me out, everyone had said I was going to end up living on the streets with the street kids, and I recall being quite scared at the thought. I had always imagined them as being very different and more dangerous. I discovered they were nothing like that. They were great kids with similar problems as mine, and I felt a real connection with them. I made the decision to keep going back to visit them. Consequently, I met a lot more kids like them.

One night as I was hanging around a mall, I met a chick named Shazza. She was rough as guts. Shazza wore a blue denim jacket with rock-band patches on the back, tight black jeans, and black desert boots. She was the oldest streetie (slang for street kid), and all the other kids looked up to her. That night I did not plan to go back to the hostel, but cops apprehended me after they name-checked me. They returned me to the hostel in the early hours of the morning.

I liked hanging around with the street kids. I felt very drawn to them, and they felt like family. Each time I went to town I walked around a few streets until I met up with one of them. It usually was not long before we met up with the others.

The next day I found myself back in town, drinking with some kids at a small lake in the landscaping between freeways. I was drunk and it was getting dark. We started heading back to town, but when we got there, we saw heaps of people outside the movie theatre, cops everywhere. It was going on eleven o'clock.

Shazza spotted me staggering around, barely able to stand. She looked up at the town clock, and going by the look on her face, she realized I should have been back at the hostel. The cops were name-checking everyone. One asked me who I was and where I lived. They got on the radio, and before I knew it, Shazza was helping them throw me in the back of the van, which then took me back to the hostel.

Once we arrived at the hostel, I waited for the cops to leave and then jumped through the kitchen window, breaking the screen. I ran all the way back to town and the malls.

It wasn't long before Shazza saw me and grabbed me by the scruff of the neck. "What are you doing here, girl? Didn't they take you home?" she yelled crossly.

I couldn't really answer her. I was afraid of what she might do to me.

"I don't know, you silly girl!" She lectured and shoved me to one side before walking off.

"Hey, Angel, what are you doing?" Moxie, who had spotted me, yelled.

When I looked up at the town clock, I saw it was going on midnight.

"We're going to the drop-in centre. You want to come get a feed?" All the streeties would go to this place. The back entrance was in a dark, dirty laneway between a bank and a restaurant. There were paintings and murals all over the walls. The hallway led to a huge room full of tables and chairs.

I watched Moxie go up to a window in the wall, where she asked for a pasty with sauce. I did the same.

"Can I please have a sausage roll?"

"Sure, you want sauce?"

"Yes please," I replied. The guy serving handed me the plate, and I went and sat next to Moxie.

"What is this place?" I asked.

"It's a drop-in centre for homeless kids. It opens at midnight. You come in, get a feed, and then you can go to the office and one of the workers will have a yarn with you. They'll give you a blanket and foam mattress that you can sleep on until six o'clock!"

"What happens at six?" I asked.

"Everyone has to leave the premises. You're lucky it's summertime, because it's freezing and still dark outside when it's winter."

All night long I heard kids coming and going as I lay on my mattress next to Moxie. Just as I dozed off, I heard a voice singing out, "Everybody up, rise and shine; it's time to go!"

We were all a little slow to respond. Some of the kids had only just come in and found it difficult to wake up because they were intoxicated. Eventually we all staggered out into the deserted city.

Wow! What a night! I had just spent the night with the street kids. I wondered what sort of trouble I was in back at the hostel—not that I really cared. I had no desire to return there.

I thought I would feel better living on the streets (and I did). However, little did I know what living on the streets was going to mean. On top of that, it was only a few days later that I collided head-on with the law.

One of the streeties' favourite pastimes was stealing cars and getting into high-speed chases with the cops. We stole cars in order to get from one break-and-enter to another, and sometimes we stole cars just for fun. I remember how we stole seven Commodores, all in one night, from all across the city, with one of the cars destroyed later in a smash-up derby.

The five street kids I hung out with thrived on deliberately getting themselves into high-speed chases. They were considered pros by the rest of us. These kids were real daredevils and seemed to have no fear, having competitions to see who was the quickest at stealing a car. The winner was always the same guy, with only four seconds from popping the lock to starting the engine. Those of us who tagged along were joyriders. It was all pretty full-on, not to mention dangerous, and there were times I thought I was going to die in a head-on smash.

One particular night in the summer of 1986, around ten o'clock, the boys, Moxie, and I were joyriding in a stolen SS Commodore. We'd had it for several days and were using it for break-and-enters. The Commodore was red hot for the cops. We had been out in the suburbs partying with some other kids and were on our way back to the city. Coming up to a red light, I freaked out when I noticed a cop car on the opposite side of the intersection. They were indicating right, turning into our lane, which meant they were now behind and following us. Our driver deliberately slowed down to let the cops get a glimpse of our number plate. I panicked because it was obvious he wanted a chase. Our driver knew the cops would soon be on their radios asking for a license check of our vehicle. Our driver suggested we lock our doors and fasten our seat belts.

The V8 motor of the stolen SS Commodore rumbled, and our driver dropped it back to a lower gear, causing the wheels to spin as we sped off from the cop car, which was now behind us. Seconds later the sirens began to sound and the chase was on. I know the cops had called for backup because out of the corner of my eye, I saw the flashing lights of other cop cars and heard their sirens everywhere. They were on either side of us, in the next block, driving parallel in the same direction at high speed. It looked as though they were trying to get in front of us to block us. This was freaky, not to mention adrenalin-pumping. We were pushing 160 kilometres per hour, and there was not much slowing down round corners. It felt like one of those sideshow rides that you wish you had never gotten on. I remember thinking, *I'm going to die, or we'll get caught, and then who will bail me out?*

Our driver had a good track record of losing the cops and getting away, but that did not stop me thinking the worst. Above the sound of sirens was a lot of yelling inside the car about where to go. He was clearly getting ready to dump the car and make a run for it. His instructions to the rest of us were, "Whatever happens we stay staunch, and if we get away, we meet up at the train station." (To stay staunch meant we were to admit to nothing, no matter what the cops said or did if they apprehended us.)

Suddenly our driver got ahead of the cops, just far enough to lock up the Commodore in the driveway of someone's home. We all jumped out, dodging rosebushes, anxious to find somewhere to hide. We bolted for the backyard and came face to face with a very high fence. I had to think fast as I was not able to jump it. Moxie had no trouble, but she paused in her escape, jumping back down from the fence in order to give me a boost up. Despite her efforts it was no use; the fence was just too high for me. Moxie had to keep going without me.

I took off my blue flannelette shirt in the hope the cops would not recognize me. Plucking up courage, I walked casually back out onto the street, walking along as if I knew nothing. A cop car drove into the street and I became nervous. They had a bright flashlight on the roof of their car that lit up all the houses as they looked for us.

They got closer and I grew more anxious. I was scared of what their response might be when they saw me. Incredibly, they drove straight past. I waited a few seconds before turning round to see if they had stopped, but they hadn't and were continuing with their search. Maybe they hadn't been expecting one of us to be casually walking along the street.

Once the cops had gone past, I decided the time had come to leg it before they came back. I ran as fast as I could to the nearest train station, the sound of sirens wailing in the distance. When I got to the station, it was deserted. Only one light was working. I remember it flickering erratically, as if it was about to blow its bulb.

I walked about the area, wondering where the others were. Suddenly, in a dark corner, I came across Moxie and the boys.

"Shh!" Moxie gestured when she saw my startled look.

They were all holding their breath and waiting anxiously, half-expecting the cops might still find them. They were as surprised to see me as I was to see them, and we chuckled quietly, relieved about our desperate but successful escape. Moxie gave me a bear hug, a huge smile on her face.

"We thought you were gone, Angel," she whispered.

I told her I had thought the same thing.

All of us felt ten feet tall and bullet proof that night. While we waited for the train (it could not come fast enough), the boys were each telling their side of the heroic getaway, with our driver bragging mostly about his spectacular Peter Brock-style of driving.

Life on the streets had its ups and downs, but it was early days for me, and so far I was enjoying every bit of it. It beat sitting around in a hostel full of people who did not know me—and as far as I was concerned did not care. On the streets I felt special; I was someone important. The public feared us, and we did whatever we wanted.

When the cops came after us, the chase was half the fun. The adrenalin rush was out of this world. Each time we got away from the cops, it added to our egos, and we would pay out on them for not being able to catch us. They were mad that we were bad. We had no care or respect for the law, and the law had it in for us.

There was no child protection in my juvenile delinquency days. Cops would use different methods in their efforts to get information out of street kids they picked up. Some of the boys on the streets recalled getting the phone book across the head if they didn't give the cops the information they wanted. I remember one particular incident where an off-duty officer spotted us during a break-and-enter. He called for backup after we ran away from him. The cops searched the area for hours before finding me, blocks away, trying to get out of the suburb.

I was taken to the local police station for questioning, but I refused to say anything. One officer got so mad he kicked my feet out from under me, causing me to fall on my hands, which were cuffed behind me at the time. I experienced excruciating pain, not to mention humiliation.

They would try everything to get information out of us. They would tell lies about what our *coo-ees* (friends/mates) had said and make false statements to get us to admit to the crimes. However, no matter what they said or did, we remained staunch.

The cops got so desperate for information we found ourselves getting harassed and picked up for questioning every day. In the end we had no choice but to complain to a higher authority. We were told there was nothing that could be done regarding how we were treated during interrogations; all we could do was take note of the officers' names and rank numbers. Once such officers had accumulated a certain number of ticks against them, then there would be an investigation. I believe that our complaints contributed largely to the formation of a youth justice committee in the early 1990s, which stands by delinquent children when they get in trouble with the law.

CHAPTER THREE

"Bunji Park"

One morning, as we were leaving the drop-in centre, my friend Moxie asked if I wanted to go for a walk to see someone about a loan. We had to go to a particular street, which was just over a train bridge, separating the suburb from the CBD (central business district). A la carte restaurants and posh nightclubs laced both sides of this street, attracting people from all walks of life. The street was also popular with members of the gay community. A couple of the nightclubs were their favourite hangouts. These nightclubs had drag queen entertainment for members only after midnight.

Right at the end of the street was a local park. Sadly, it was there that many young girls sold their bodies illegally for money. The park was also home to many homeless members of the Indigenous community. I became very fond of some of them. They were responsible for giving the park the nickname *Bunji Park,* and the men hanging round it were called *bunji men*—men who drove around the park looking for sexual favours from these girls.

It was in this park that I met Raven, who had been on the scene since she was nine years old. Raven would stay all over the place, sometimes at women's refuges but most times in motels, which she was able to use after her clients (bunji men) had finished using them. Over time we became close friends.

We really enjoyed each other's company. Raven loved to smoke marijuana. We would often sit together in the park, soaking up the sun while smoking a big three-papery joint, enjoying ourselves and laughing. We would do this every day while Raven would wait for her regular clients to come driving around the park. When they did she would walk over to the car and jump in, and they would drive off. Raven would be away for half an hour to an hour, tops. I would anxiously wait for her return. It was sad to watch all this. Raven hated it, and I hated that she had to do it, but at the end of the day it was all she knew, the only way she had to survive.

Raven was saving to go visit her family. Her baby sister was turning five, and she was desperate to go see her. Tears welled up in Raven's eyes when she spoke of her family and how much she missed them. She had not been back to see them in a long time. I remember strongly urging her one night to go and see her family as soon as she could, and she made the decision to leave the next morning.

"See you when you get back!" I yelled as I ran alongside the moving bus. Once it had gone, I walked back over the bridge to the CBD.

A week later I was walking back to the park to see if Raven had returned from her family visit when I ran into friends, Roxy and Shorty. They were cashed up from doing break-and-enters all day and were planning to party at the casino all night.

"We're going back to my place to get ready. You want to come with us, Angel?" Shorty asked.

"Yeah, sounds mad, but how are we getting there?"

"We've got a stolen car parked at the old hotel. We'll jump in that—hey?"

"No way, that's hot as! We're better off catching a cab. It's safer!" I said.

While we were getting ready, we had a few drinks, giving us the courage to walk into the casino (we were all underage). As Roxy and I were playing the game of two-up, two brothers approached us. Their names were Gunner and Hunter.

Gunner and Hunter were from my old suburb. They were half-cast Indigenous boys with fair complexions. Both good-looking boys, but from what I could remember, they were crazy. You did not want to mess with them. They had a reputation like no one else, which explained why Shorty took off the minute he saw them coming.

Gunner was eyeing Roxy when he invited us back to their table beside the dance floor. We drank and danced all night, and before we knew it, it was five in the morning and time to go home—wherever that was. Gunner and Roxy looked inseparable. Gunner suggested we go back to their place for a session of *gunja* (marijuana) and some bacon and eggs.

The two boys lived at home with their mum, Chase, and their three-year-old sister, Ash. When their mum heard Roxy and I were street kids, she offered us a room to rent. She was kind like that. I gladly accepted her offer as a break from the streets. We were able to pay some rent out of the allowance we received from government Welfare.

Gunner and Roxy were tight, and Roxy had no plans of leaving him anytime soon. In the meantime, I made myself useful by cooking and cleaning, as I was very domesticated. I felt the need to help the family while I stayed with them.

Their home was in our old suburb not far from my parents' place. It also happened to be just across the road from my old high school. It dawned on me that both of my younger sisters were attending the primary school there. I hadn't seen them in ages, so I decided to make contact.

I visited my sisters every day during their lunch break, until my mum found out and threatened to call the cops if I ever went there again. Days later my mother informed me they were moving to Italy for good. My parents feared that if they stayed in Australia, what had happened to me would happen to my sisters.

This news devastated me, to say the least. It shocked me to think I was going to be left on my own in Australia without any family at all. Feelings of total abandonment overwhelmed me. The thought I might never see them again constantly gnawed at me.

When the day of their departure arrived, I stole a car and drove to the international airport to see them off, only to discover they had flown out some days before. That night I drank and cried myself to sleep, while Gunner and Hunter kept assuring me that as far as they were concerned, I was part of *their* family now.

Gunner and Hunter became the brothers I never had. We did everything together—stealing cars, break-and-entering sprees across the suburbs, and parties that never ended. We even got caught up in gang wars between other Indigenous families.

Because of this, I had to be taught how to fight the dirty street-fighting way, where there were no rules, and weapons were involved. Gunner's technique involved teaching me how to have my guard up at all times, ready for the punch that he was going to throw at me. His punches would usually come when I wasn't expecting them. If I were not quick enough to block them, I would wear them.

"Guard up!" he said repeatedly. I knew it was his way of "training" me, but sometimes it felt as if I was in some kind of prison camp—a camp where I was stabbed, choked, and violently bullied on a regular basis, all in the name of "we can't be beaten."

I began to wonder if Gunner hated me, to be hurting me so much. Yet when Roxy and I found ourselves in threatening situations, Gunner and Hunter were always there to protect us, no matter how big and scary the opposition. These two guys were truly buff.

It was 1987 and every day was a party at Gunner and Hunter's home as we were always cashed-up after a day's work of crime. We truly were living destructive lifestyles.

During our crime sprees, Gunner became closely acquainted with an Indigenous fellow named Spider, who was the local drug dealer in our suburb. (Spider was twelve years older and claimed to be related to Gunner and Hunter's family.)

The time came when Gunner got busted again and landed back in juvenile detention. This was his second home if not his first, for he spent most of his time locked up.

It was August, and one night, while Roxy and I were babysitting her little sister, Ash, a car pulled into the driveway. It was Hunter and his homeys, returning from a night out on the piss.

They barged in through the front door, Spider following close behind.

"Hey, girls. Where's Mum?" Hunter asked.

"She's at the casino with a date," Roxy replied.

Spider immediately walked over and sat beside me. He was playing with a screwdriver in a way that was making me really nervous.

Hunter took Roxy by the hand, leading her toward the bedrooms. This left me sitting alone with Spider.

Suddenly, without any warning, Spider lashed out, stabbing me viciously in the leg with the screwdriver before dragging me outside, where he raped me. I was in complete shock.

Spider asked if what he was doing was love or rape. I said nothing. I was quietly crying as I stared into the dark, starry sky. I was too afraid to say anything in case of what he might do next.

When he was done, Spider got up and went back into the house, acting as if nothing had happened.

I was scared for Roxy, but she was with Hunter, so I knew she would be safe. I quickly gathered my things and locked myself in the toilet until the boys' mum got back.

I questioned myself as to why Hunter did not try to stop Spider. Gunner and Hunter had always protected me. This would not have happened if Gunner had been there, no way in hell! All I could put it down to was that Hunter must have been scared of Spider, which seemed unusual because these boys were not scared of anyone.

As I reasoned within myself, I cried, nursing the stab wound in my leg, covering the wound with toilet paper. Suddenly I heard a car pull into the driveway. It was Chase, their mum.

When she came inside, I heard her asking Roxy where I was. I unlocked the toilet door and slowly crept out.

"What's wrong?" Chase asked.

As I told her what had happened, a horrified look came over her face.

"Please don't tell anyone," I pleaded. I was shaking with nerves.

Chase protested. "We have to call the police. He can't get away with this. He's been doing this to other girls for years."

I was very scared because I knew what would happen if the police got involved. Spider had a big family, and if he were charged, I would have to answer to them. I would be forever living in fear for my life.

"No! Just call a doctor if you want, but no police!" I insisted, terrified.

The doctor came, checked me over, and prescribed a sedative to calm me down. Not long after I had dozed off, I was woken by the sound of shouting and loud banging on the front door.

Bang, bang, bang! "Open up! Police! Open this door!"

I could barely walk, and when I opened the front door, they charged in, yelling, "Where is he?"

I was overwhelmed, confused by all the commotion. I thought I was dreaming, as I was groggy from the sedative. Before I could ask "who", they were dragging Spider from one of the bedrooms, where he must have crashed after doing what he did to me.

I was horrified that he was still in the house, sleeping as though nothing had happened. I watched on in greater horror as they dragged him outside and into the paddy wagon (what a police vehicle was called at the time).

The detective came back to me. "Are you the young lass reportedly raped tonight?"

"Umm, yes, but how did you find out?"

"We received a phone call, so get dressed and come with us so you can give us a statement."

I was so angry. Chase had gone against my wishes. I looked around, but she had locked herself in her room.

I got dressed and went with them. I had no choice in the matter. They were a special unit, dealing with major incidents.

I was there from midnight until five in the morning, as they wanted to know every little detail.

They had my used tampon and underpants in a clip-top bag as evidence, and now they were taking me to a sexual-assault referral centre where they took swabs for evidence and photos of my stab wound. I felt so humiliated and sick inside that I wanted to die.

A woman counsellor took me into a little room, sat me down, and asked how I was feeling mentally, physically, and emotionally. They were amazed at how bravely I was dealing with such a horrific attack, but when the counsellor asked me to tell her a little more about it, I broke down in tears. We both realized I was not as strong as everyone thought I was.

The next morning I was taken back to Gunner and Hunter's home. No one was about, and even if there had been, I was too tired to deal with Chase or anyone else. I just crashed out on my bed.

Suddenly I was jolted awake by a guy punching me in the face and threatening me with a bounty on my head. As he continued to pummel me, he told me Spider was being charged with rape as well as "deprivation of liberty."

"Who are you?" I cried, trying desperately to protect my face.

"I'm his little brother," he said angrily.

This attack was only the first. There were many more to come.

I had no choice but to flee the house, leaving Roxy behind. From that night on I would wipe myself out, knowing I would not feel a thing if someone blew my head off.

Later that night I found myself sitting in Bunji Park, totally wasted and hoping Raven would soon jump out of a client's car. All of a sudden three huge Indigenous women surrounded me, catching me off guard. They claimed to be related to Spider and were telling me, in very loud, colourful terms, what they thought of me. Out of nowhere came a hard punch to my head, then another, and before I knew it, I was down on the ground with one on top and the other two kicking me in the ribs. I finally managed to overcome the one on top of me.

When they saw I was gaining the upper hand they bolted off in to the night. I got up, screaming, "You black f*cks, come back!" But they were gone.

I staggered around the park, in disbelief at what had just happened. Yet I was not entirely surprised. I had expected repercussions of this kind.

My shirt was torn and I was splattered with blood. I heard a car door slamming in the distance. It was dark and difficult to see.

I called out across the park. "Raven, is that you?"

"Angel?"

As Raven got closer, she realized something was wrong.

"Oh my God, what happened to you? Are you okay?"

Raven held my face up to the light of the moon.

"Who did this to you, and where have you been?" she kept asking, adding, "I've been looking for you for weeks."

I did not say anything, as I did not know where to start. So much had happened since I had waved Raven good-bye. In that moment, all I could do was cry.

"That's it. I'm not leaving your side ever again, girl. Let's go get you cleaned up and then we'll get stoned. No more drinking for you, we'll just get smashed on cones."

Raven took me back to her motel, where she ran me a warm bath. While I was in the bath, Raven rang a women's hostel, telling them about my rape and recent attack. I overheard her making arrangements for me to stay there. Raven told me it was a nice, safe place, adding that it was out of harm's way. She was worried for me and felt that if I stayed on the streets, the chances were very high of more attacks.

In the morning, after I had secured my place at the refuge, we went out. Raven was cashed-up, and it was payday for me—the special allowance for homeless youth, paid $144 every fortnight and it was my shout.

Raven led the way through lanes and alleyways before coming to a halt at an old wooden gate. This led to the back door of a house where Axel, Raven's dope dealer, lived.

Axel answered the door in nothing more than a singlet and an old pair of ruggers. He wore glasses and had earrings in both ears. His grey hair was tied up in a ponytail. When Axel spoke, he had a strong English accent, which I found very amusing.

"Raven, my darling, come in," he insisted.

You could smell the sweet scent of incense burning as we walked into his home. Axel put the kettle on while Raven rolled a big three-papery joint that she passed around. I didn't smoke that much, but I still felt wasted as I sat looking around the place.

They were both chatting away when I saw him hand Raven two syringes and a little clip-top bag containing a small amount of white powder. My eyes lit up as I had only ever heard about this stuff.

Raven turned to me, waving the bag in the air. "Here, Angel, we'll go halves, hey?"

I had adrenalin rushing through my body before she was even ready to inject me.

I had never used a needle before, so I did not quite know what to expect. I watched Raven as she carefully inserted the needle into my vein. I instantly felt a rush go through my entire body, from my groin to the ends of my hair. It felt like my hair was standing on end, and my heart began to beat really fast. I had to admit it felt good compared to everything else that was going on in my life. Yet in the middle of the rush, my conscience was loudly screaming "*No!*"

Raven and I stayed together all the time, but we would separate at those times when she was soliciting in the park. I felt very guilty about her selling her body to support our needs, and I have to admit at times I felt tempted to do the same, but I did not have the guts to do it. I would hear my conscience scream at the thought of it. Not only that, Raven warned me to never work at the park because if I did she would kill me.

Deep down Raven hated what she was doing and would show it in the way she treated her clients. I would watch in horror as Raven kicked clients' cars, punched them in the face through their driver windows, and screamed profanities at them as they drove off. There was nothing they could do about it, as they knew what they were doing was illegal, as did Raven.

Raven was full of anger knowing this was the only way she had to support herself, even though it was highly risky and could lead to incarceration if she were caught.

It was going on six o'clock and getting dark when Raven and I separated one evening. I took off to the nearest bottle shop while she went off to do her thing.

I was drinking in a squat nearby with some Indigenous friends when we noticed we had run out of drink. That was when I decided to scab some more money from the bunji men, who were hanging around the park. I was doing really well until one of them held out a crisp one hundred-dollar bill. I had been scabbing money from this same person for months, and this time I was a little too drunk to say no to what he was asking of me.

The next morning I woke feeling dirty and guilty. I was overwhelmed with sadness at what I had done.

I drank excessively to block out the guilt and used what Spider had done to me as an excuse to justify my actions. I was already in depression from his attack, and this just made things a whole lot worse. I lost all respect for myself and did not care anymore.

In order to cope, I switched my mind off, refusing to acknowledge it. I endured by wiping myself out on whatever I could get my hands on and hid away from all my streetie friends, crying on the shoulders of drugs and alcohol. I was drowning in misery and grief. It got to the point where I desperately looked for comfort from the God who had comforted me once before—a God I knew existed and who seemed interested in me regardless of my lifestyle or my circumstances.

Days later, Raven and I were at the refuge centre. It was too hot to go anywhere, and we decided to laze around on the back deck under the shade of a big old willow tree. We were just having a cigarette when the phone rang and one of the workers came out, handing me the phone.

I put the receiver to my ear. "Hello?"

A voice on the other end threatened my life if I testified against Spider at the trial. The caller then hung up but rang back a few seconds later.

Raven snatched the phone from me, intending to give the caller a piece of her mind, but she went quiet as she listened to what was being said.

When the call finished, Raven passed on the message. "Apparently, Spider is in jail. The inmates are on a hunger strike and rioting over poor living conditions. They threaten that if Spider dies, so do you."

These threatening calls shook me up. I wondered how they had known to call that number. I began to panic, fretting for my life and my family's lives. I told the people at the refuge centre that I was leaving. They advised me not to. They believed I would be safer there with them. However, they did not know this mob as I did. I was sure that if I stayed, the house would be "rocked" with bricks flying through windows, or worse still, there could be a home invasion. I did not want to put the other women in the house at risk of being seriously hurt. Raven seemed worried too.

It all seemed like a bad dream, a nightmare from which I could not wake up.

That afternoon I was back on the streets, walking everywhere with my head held low, but as the days passed by, I would often get intercepted by groups of two or three members of the Indigenous community, who would promptly begin bashing me. These bashings ended up becoming a daily occurrence. I constantly wore bruises and black eyes. The only way I could block out the pain was to drink myself numb every day.

One night a group of ten of them walked into the drop-in centre. They were looking for me. All the streeties stood in front of me. We were twenty to their ten. The group left, swearing and threatening that at some point they would get me alone.

I felt as though I was the bad guy and Spider was the victim. I was also very angry with Chase for calling the cops that night. I had known it would reap these kinds of results.

That night I lay on my mattress, thinking of a way to stop all the madness, and I decided to write Spider a letter.

"Dear Spider,

My name is Angel. You might not remember me, but I am the girl you stabbed and raped that night. I am writing because your family will not leave me alone. They are constantly bashing me for what *you* did, and the truth is you deserve to be where you are. I didn't call the cops. It was Chase. I want you to tell your family to leave me alone and take the matter up with her. I also want you

30

to know that as angry as I am about what you did, I forgive you. —Angel."

This was the most stupid thing I could have done, because Spider's lawyer used that letter against me at the trial, and the prosecutor had me for lunch. As a result, Spider's sentence was lowered from six years to four, with a two-year minimum with parole.

The bashings continued.

Life on the streets was taking its toll on me physically and emotionally. I was becoming angrier and angrier, closing myself off behind a brick wall. This was my survival strategy to keep people out so I could not get hurt.

I was drunk every single night and committing crimes, crimes I could not remember the next day. Stealing cars enabled me to get to parties that were far from the city centre.

One particular night, after realizing I had been at the same house drunk for two whole days, I decided I had better make my way back to the city. The uncle of a girlfriend offered me a lift. There were three of us in the car—the uncle, his friend, and me. We were just about to hit the freeway heading south when the uncle spun his car around and started heading in the opposite direction.

"We're going the wrong way!" I shouted.

The uncle replied by saying that they had to pick something up from the other person's place. Desperate, I opened the car door, intending to jump out.

"Are you crazy?" the uncle asked, speeding faster and faster.

Tears welled up in my eyes. Jumping out of that speeding car could very well kill me; I just couldn't bring myself to do it. So despite my very deep fear of what the uncle might be planning for me, I remained where I was.

Before long we were driving in a forested area on the outskirts of the city. There were many rumours about this place, and I was petrified as to why we were there. Suddenly the car came to a complete stop on the wet and boggy road. The uncle tried to reverse the car, but it was well and truly bogged.

The uncle got out of the car, demanding I get out and push because the guy in the passenger seat had crashed out drunk. That was when I made a run for it, but the uncle caught me and dragged me back to the car. The interior light came on as he shoved me back inside. I took the opportunity to get a good look at his face so I would remember what he looked like.

"Take a good look. I've only just gotten out of the can, and I really don't give a f*ck about anything," he snarled.

I swallowed hard, terrified I was not going to get out of the forest alive. That was when an idea came to my mind. I figured that if I could convince the bloke I was a prostitute, he would not feel as if he had to kill me once he was finished with me.

I dried my eyes and took a deep breath of courage before telling him I would service him for free if he would drop me back in town. His excuse was that he did not have enough petrol, but I assured him I would give him a hundred dollars if he took me back to my destination. He stared at me in disbelief and I smiled back. I needed to convince him I was okay with it all, as if I did this sort of stuff all the time. As I got my act on, I sensed him calming down. He reached into his pocket and ripped out a condom. I thanked God he had one.

Straight after he had what he wanted from me, I encouraged him to get us out of the bog so we could go and get the cash I had promised him. He nudged his friend to get up. Once the big guy was up and pushing the car, we were soon out of the bog and heading back to town.

I couldn't wait to get back to the city and was on tenterhooks the whole drive back. Once we were in the city, I directed them to the park. The moment he stopped the car, I was out, bolting away as fast as I could—out of sight, out of mind. I didn't have the courage to look behind me. I just kept running until I couldn't run anymore. When I eventually stopped, I braced myself and cried deep tears as the realization hit that I could easily have been killed in that forest.

I never told anyone except Raven about it. I had no interest in telling the cops, as I was ashamed this had happened to me again. This event affected my soul in a way nothing else had up to that point. I could have died, and who would have known or cared?

Over time I let my heart become as hard as petrified wood. Like a wild, untamed animal I protected myself from further hurt by wearing a shield of hostility. This hostility was plain to see, for I became very aggressive in my manners and attitudes. My probation officer once told me I came across to her as a very scary young girl.

Surprisingly, I was shocked when she said this because *deep down* that was not how I wanted to come across—I *wanted* to love. This was impossible, however, if I were to survive the wild environment and conditions in which I lived.

CHAPTER FOUR

A New Creation

It was midnight, and the doors of the drop-in centre were opening. I had convinced Raven to come with me to get a feed. I had not seen anyone else for weeks.

While we were there, I met a girl named Shirl, who called herself a Christian. She was attending a church in the city. Shirl was showing boldness when she asked me if I knew who Jesus was.

"Yeah, I know God!" I retorted.

We talked a bit along those lines, and then she asked me to go for a walk. She told me there was someone she wanted me to meet. We reached a building with a sign that indicated it was a church.

Once inside, she led me to the back of the building, which was decked out like a granny flat. A man was sitting there with a book in hand and candles burning all around. I was pinching myself to see if I was awake because this was quite bizarre.

He got up and introduced himself while he shook my hand. He offered us a cold drink as we sat and talked. "Shirl tells me you talk a lot about God. Would you like to know Him more?"

I nodded and then waited for him to do something weird, like begin chanting or praying some weird prayer. Instead, he told me to close my eyes and repeat a prayer after him, which I did, opening one eye to see what he was doing. He called it the salvation prayer—which one prayed in order to be born again and make Jesus the Lord of one's life.

This was strange to me. I had never heard anything like this, and I had been going to church most of my life! I also believed I was saying yes to a God I already knew existed.

The prayer went something like this: "Heavenly Father, I come to You in the name of Jesus, and I confess I have sinned against You. Forgive me. I believe Your Son, Jesus Christ, died on the cross to pay for my sin and rose from the dead on the third day. He is alive today, and I put my faith and trust only in Jesus Christ to forgive and save me from the penalty of my sin. I confess Jesus as my Lord and Saviour and I receive His precious gift of eternal life. Thank You for loving me; I thank You for it in Jesus's name, amen."

After the prayer, he and Shirl hugged me and congratulated me, telling me I was now a child of God. He handed me a Bible, inviting me to come along to a Sunday service, which would take place in that building.

As I walked back to the drop-in centre I thought hard about what had happened and the things he had said. I wondered if I was meant to feel *different* because I sure wasn't *feeling* any different. Maybe it was because I was already sure in my heart that God was watching over me. He had proven that, through His powerful presence, which surrounded me each day.

Days later I found myself waiting for Raven in a local pub, in order to score a stick, which was a $20 deal of marijuana wrapped in foil. It was early, and the pub hadn't been open for business very long. The only person in the bar was a woman who had just walked in a few minutes earlier. The woman went off to use the facilities and a short while later came out and sat beside me. She was chatting away with the barmaid when she quickly glanced at me and asked if I was with Raven. I smiled and nodded. She then introduced herself as Brook and said she was also waiting to score from Raven.

Brook was very open, telling me her life story of how she was a thirty-six-year-old single mum with two small boys who were both in primary school.

"How about you?" she asked.

After learning I was a homeless street kid, she was shocked and kindly offered me a place to stay. I sensed she was feeling sorry for me.

When Raven got back, we all went to Brook's for the day. She lived in a government housing unit in a suburb a good twenty minutes from the city. We had a great day, and she seemed nice enough, easy going—I accepted her offer to stay.

After I had been living with Brook for four months, it was clear she was having a positive impact on me. I found myself living a lot healthier, eating three square meals a day and sober most of the time. I was even getting lots of exercise because her unit was near a huge public oval where we would kick a ball around with her two boys. Her boys were so much fun that at times I felt like I was a kid again.

It was in this sober state that I found myself thinking about my life. With no family to call my own, I wondered what lay ahead and where I would go from there. I was not seeing much of Raven anymore, as it was a good twenty minutes by transport from the city, but she stayed in touch by phoning regularly.

Early one morning Raven rang to inform me that Funny, one of the street kids, was asking for me. He wanted my address so he could write to me. When I finally received his letter, he informed me that he was going to the East Coast to live with his dad. It was either that or twelve months in a boys home for break-and-entering charges. He went on to say that if I was ever interested in going east, I was welcome to stay with them anytime.

I paused from reading Funny's letter and thought about the opportunity to get out of the city and start fresh somewhere else. It sounded like the perfect escape route, but how would I get there?

I remembered how Roxy and I had worked for an old guy named Irish a few summers ago. It had been seasonal work doing concrete and pebble paving. I decided to visit Irish and ask him for a job. My ticket to the East Coast was going to cost $271 one way. If I could get a few weeks' work with Irish, I would be able to get there.

I knew they would be difficult weeks because Irish was not an ordinary old man—he was a grumpy old Irishman with huge issues. He was tall, and his walk reminded me of a giant in a nursery rhyme—fee-fi-fo-fum, etc. Despite some misgivings I knocked loudly on his gate.

"Who's that?" he yelled.

"It's me, Angel!" I replied.

He was in constant fear of someone robbing him, and he used big locks on his front gate. Irish met me at the gate, and I tried to guess what his mood was.

"Long time no see! How you been, young Angel?" he asked, unlocking his gate. "What brings you here today? Have a seat. Would you like a beer?" He pulled a tinny from the fridge.

"Yes thanks, that'll be great," I replied. "I was wondering if you had some work as I'm in need of some quick cash."

"Well," he said, "I've got another fellow on at the moment. He's Italian, like you. I could probably squeeze you in, yeah."

His backyard was clearly being renovated and he went on. "I could probably give you some work Saturdays too. You could lay some tiles here on the patio. Do you think you could do a bit of tiling?"

"I've never done it before but I'm keen to learn."

"Good! You have a job. I'll pick you up at four sharp. You'll be ready?"

"Yes, sir," I replied and sculled the rest of my beer. "Well, I'm off to get an early night. Good night, and thanks heaps."

"See ya then, young Angel!"

I let myself out through the heavy gate.

Working with Irish was not easy. He got cranky if things did not go his way, and he confused me by calling everything a *bizzo*. He yelled at me in a raging fit if I did not know what he meant when he shouted, "Get that bizzo and put it over this bizzo here!" Everything was a bizzo. I managed to get two weeks' work out of him before finally getting a kick up the butt and being told where to go!

The tickets were booked. It was December 1989, and I was set to leave. I was turning seventeen.

The cops were always reminding me that I was getting closer to going to an adults jail, seeing I had only one year left before I turned eighteen. They would say that the boys and girls homes were nothing compared to a women's jail. They would add that they couldn't wait until they could lock me up in there.

"But what if I don't do anything wrong?" I asked.

"Oh, we'll find something," they replied.

Going by that, I knew I had to get away. Besides, what was keeping me? It was not as if my family was going to return from Italy anytime soon.

In addition, according to the magistrate, I had blown all my chances as a juvenile delinquent. It clearly wouldn't take much before I was locked up again. Going on all of this, moving to the East Coast never sounded better.

One week before I was set to leave, I called a friend of the family, telling him I was leaving town, just in case my family were ever looking for me. He then informed me that my dad had arrived from Italy just the day before. He put my dad on the phone, and we arranged to meet up.

When my dad arrived, he did not want to come inside the apartment, so we sat in the car overlooking the oval. I had mixed feelings and didn't know what to say.

"Dad, I'm moving to the East Coast in a couple of days."

"Why don't you come with me back to Italy?" he asked.

It felt good to know my dad still wanted me in his life, but I feared that if I went and things did not work out, I would have nowhere to run.

"Sorry, I can't, Dad. I wouldn't feel good going there. I'm off to start a new life."

Dad seemed saddened by my response but then erupted in anger. "You'll end up in the gutter, my friend!"

I quickly got out and stood beside the car, scared of what he might do next. I felt so sad. I knew he was hurting, but I was hurting too.

"Bye, Dad. I love you. I'll keep in touch."

My dad wept as he drove off. I was crying too, his last words playing repeatedly in my head.

I walked back through the front door, overwhelmed with sadness and wondering whether I would ever see him again. Brook knew by looking at me that a drink was definitely in the cards. She watched me reach for a glass and the half-empty bottle of scotch, which I drank until I couldn't feel the pain in my heart anymore.

I woke to the sound of the clock alarm and was soon packed and ready to go. My journey was going to be a long one. Brook and a few other mates drove me to the bus depot.

Roo, a good friend, walked me onto the bus playing his didgeridoo. He handed me $20. "Take care, sis; it's been nice knowing you."

Brook jumped on the bus and gave me a hug. She handed me $20 as well as sleeping tablets, telling me, "You're going to need them."

During the bus journey, I had a real chance to mull over things and get in touch with my inner self. Part of me felt sad to be leaving while another part felt scared not knowing where I was going or what to expect. Funny had said he would meet me, but I was worried he would not be there when I arrived. I was fearful and nervous to say the least, but I found peace when I turned to God, drawing near to Him for comfort.

The bus stopped three times a day for twenty-minute breaks for breakfast, lunch, and dinner. The money Brook and Roo had given me I wisely used for food. I took sleeping tablets in the evenings so I could get some sleep, but not before soaking in the beautiful sunsets over our amazing Australian outback landscape. On the final day, I moved down to the front of the bus and grabbed a seat behind the driver.

The coast appeared. It was beautiful. I had never seen water such a turquoise blue. "Wow!" I cried, standing up as we drove past the big sign proclaiming "Welcome." People were walking along the street wearing only their bathing suits. I wanted to get off the bus right then and there.

"Where are you going?" the bus driver asked.

I told him, shouting above the sound of traffic, thinking my destination was somewhere in the vicinity.

"Sit down, young lass, you've still got some hours to go," he informed me.

"What?" I sighed and wondered whether the place was somewhere in the sticks. Another few hours meant I was going off for another sleep.

We finally arrived at seven o'clock, and Funny was waiting for me as promised. We walked to his place, where he introduced me to his family. They seemed nice enough. I wanted a beer and asked Funny if we could go for a walk to a bottle shop.

We walked through town before stopping at a pub to buy a six pack, which we drank as we sat overlooking a river. It felt strange being here, and the beer helped calm my anxiety. Compared to where I had come from, this place was a small country town with a pub on every corner. I was already feeling homesick.

After we finished drinking, we walked back to Funny's to find his sister and her boyfriend fighting. I felt weird staying where people were fighting.

"Funny, I don't want to stay here," I said.

"It's okay, it's not about you. My brother-in-law goes crazy when he drinks rum. Let's go next door to my cousin's place. It's cool!"

The next day Funny and I went sightseeing. It was his payday. We went here and there and enjoyed checking out the main shopping mall. As we walked, we talked, reminiscing about a time when we were on whizz (meth) together.

"Gee, I wouldn't mind a shot; can you score some?" I asked.

"Nah, I don't know anyone who's got any of that here."

"That sucks! I wouldn't mind some right now."

"Plenty of pot though. I can get some of that off my sister."

"Okay, whatever!" I replied.

Marijuana was not my thing, and I only indulged if I was already drunk.

Two months on and I had become familiar with the town and knew my way around. I also got to know an older woman named Jazz who worked at a nightclub, which was a local hangout for many Indigenous people. I befriended a few after being introduced by Jazz. Jazz and I got along really well, despite the fact she was three times my age.

Funny and I drifted apart when I moved into a youth hostel. This particular hostel was a great place. I felt like a kid again staying there. They took us on great adventures such as swimming at the beach, canoeing in rivers, and even a spot of fishing. The house was very spacious and even had a pool table. I liked playing pool, having learnt to play really well when I was in juvenile detention.

I gradually grew to love the area and life on the East Coast. Everything was so much greener and had a holiday atmosphere. My homesickness was finally gone, and there was hope in the knowledge that I could not just go get a shot of whizz whenever the urge came on.

CHAPTER FIVE

Run, Girl, Run!

It was a Saturday night, and I had plans to party at the nightclub. There were curfews at the hostel, but on weekends we were all permitted to stay out, as long as they knew we were safe. Usually we would get back by ten or would stay out with a friend. This particular night I had plans of going back to Jazz's house for the night.

I walked into the nightclub and as usual, Jazz was serving at the bar. "What will you have?"

"Give me a port first," I replied. I needed a quick fix, and port always did that. One glass later and I was feeling warm and fuzzy. Generally, I could drink anyone under the table because my tolerance was very high. I could party all night until well in to the morning and still be standing when everyone else was out cold.

We were having a good time when Jazz shouted that it was closing time. I staggered up to the bar for one last drink. Jazz gave me another beer on the house and asked me to wait outside while she finished up. I went out to the front of the club where it was crowded with drunken people waiting for cabs.

As I sat outside smoking, several fights started up. I was almost punched out a few times because I was so close to everyone. I don't know how long I was waiting, but I finally decided to go looking for Jazz. One of the other girls told me Jazz had left ten minutes prior. Maybe she hadn't seen me amongst all the people out front.

I couldn't just go back to the hostel, not in the state I was in. I needed to get to Jazz's somehow, but I could not remember how to get there. I had only been over the bridge to the north side once before when I first visited her. Luckily I remembered the name of the street so I decided to go off and find it.

I walked toward the bridge. Halfway over I heard two fellas walking quickly some distance behind me. They were Indigenous boys. I did not think much of it so I kept walking. The bridge was very long and wide. At this time of the morning, there was no traffic.

One of the boys jogged to catch up to me. I thought maybe he wanted to hit me up for a fag (cigarette).

"Hey, doll, where you going?"

"Home," I said.

"Do you want me to walk with you?"

"No, I'm okay."

I began to cross over to the other side of the bridge, trying to put distance between us, but he followed. I started to freak out because now his friend was catching up as well.

"Don't run away from me. You should let me walk you home," he said.

"I'm fine, okay?" I shouted at him.

"You'll get raped walking on your own," he insisted.

The other fellow was drawing close. I was getting really worried. There was an exit on the footpath of the bridge, leading down to a large oval. As the second fellow came up, they both grabbed me by my arms and almost carried me down the exit, to the dark oval below. I was fighting, but they ignored my struggles. They were too strong. Neither said anything. I kept screaming and trying to break away from their grip but it was no use; there was no one around, no one who could hear my cry for help. They pushed me to the ground and had their way with me. They took turns using and abusing me before finally running off, disappearing in to the night.

I cried as I lay there, wondering what was happening and why it was happening to me again.

Once they had gone, I got to my feet and began looking for my clothes and shoes. I could not see anything in front of me as it was very dark. I looked up to see which way to go, and that was when I spotted some house lights up ahead at the end of the huge oval. I walked toward them. When I got to the house, I knocked on the door and when the owners opened it, I blurted out what had happened. They immediately called the cops.

The cops came and took me to the station where they started asking me a series of questions about the attack. As they did, I remembered my first rape and all that I had gone through at the police station. I did not want to go through that again, so I told the cops I did not want to press any charges. I told them it was my own fault, as I shouldn't have been walking the streets at that time of the morning. I asked if they would just take me home.

"Are you sure we can't help you?" they asked.

"No it's all right. I can't even give you a description because I really didn't see them that well. All I know is they were both Indigenous. One guy was tall and the other was short and stocky. Please just take me home!"

"Okay, if you insist. Let us know later if you change your mind," they said.

"Sure!"

They took me to Jazz's, and when I got there, I told her what had happened. She said she had looked for me but had not been able to find me. Jazz promptly began blaming herself.

"Hey, Angel, I'm looking for someone to help around here and get my girl off to school. You could live here rent-free. What do you say? Interested?"

I was not that keen since I quite liked living at the hostel. The people and the kids there were great. However, her offer did sound tempting.

"I'll think about it!"

"Okay," she replied.

Later in the morning, Jazz went for a shower and asked if I would iron a couple of shirts for her. As I was ironing, I found myself reliving the attack of the night before and my eyes filled with tears. How could I be raped three times in one lifetime?

I was overwhelmed with emotions and tried desperately to make some sense of my life. Questions filled my head.

Why was I born to my parents?

Why was I rebellious?

Why didn't my parents love each other?

Why didn't they love me?

Why did they fight all the time?

Why, why, why?

I wanted answers! Answers as to why my life had no real meaning or purpose, and why I blindly went wherever life took me. I wondered what life would have been like if I had just stuck it out at home and put up with my parents.

No matter how long and hard I thought about everything, I knew there was nothing I could do to change any of it. What was done was done. It was time to just accept things and keep on going.

Jazz came downstairs and noticed I had been crying. "Are you okay, sweetie?" she asked, hugging me tight.

"I'll be okay," I answered.

"Back in a minute," Jazz said.

Five minutes later she was back, with a guy with long curly hair that covered his eyes. He peered through the locks of his hair, looking up at me as I was ironing. Jazz introduced us.

"Angel, meet Ziggy. Ziggy, this is Angel. She's only just arrived from the West Coast."

"Hi!" I said.

"Hi," he replied and tipped an ounce of dope on the table. That was when I figured Jazz was scoring herself a bag of weed.

"Do you want a cone?" she asked.

"No thanks."

"Want a beer then?"

"Yeah, later, Jazz," I said.

As the months went by I developed a good friendship with Ziggy. I moved in to Jazz's, and from there we saw a lot of each other.

Ziggy was delightful to be around, and I considered him a good friend. I could talk to him about anything, and he would just sit there listening. Over time I developed feelings for him. I really admired him but swore to myself I would never let him know. I was still busy building brick walls around myself.

I began to keep a check on myself, to make sure I wasn't getting too depressed. My strong-willed nature wouldn't allow me to be totally overcome by the worries of this world.

I discovered that the more I looked to God, the more I felt like a warrior who could overcome any situation that came along, no matter how bad that situation was. I also noticed that it was only when I looked to Him that strength came—an inexplicable power that enabled me to suck up my tears, take a deep breath, and look determinedly into the future in the confident hope and belief that all would be okay.

God's awesome presence would often surround and comfort me when I was alone, drinking myself to tears. Even though I *was* alone, I never actually *felt* alone because it was in these times that I experienced inner refreshing and received an inner boost to keep going.

One morning Ziggy asked me if I wanted to go for a walk with him to his place, to pick up some dope he had stashed under the house.

Ziggy, as well as everyone else, seemed to love smoking dope. It was as normal as having a coffee break. I got the impression that this was how people socialized in this town. Unlike in my hometown, where as far as I knew only few and far between smoked dope, and it was mainly for partying.

Upon arriving at Ziggy's home, I was blown away by the smell of dope that billowed out through the door when he opened it. Ziggy introduced me to his mum, Sapphire, and his brother Mack. They were both sitting at the kitchen table, his mum smoking a huge joint.

Ziggy was the oldest in his family. Besides his brother Mack, he had two younger siblings, Lola and Blue, who were out in the neighbourhood somewhere playing with friends.

After Ziggy had done his thing, we left and were walking back to Jazz's, when suddenly a young boy and girl came running up behind us singing, "Woo hoo, Ziggy's got a girlfriend!"

"Are you Ziggy's girlfriend?" the pretty girl with brown eyes asked. Both were being cheeky, smirking and giggling.

"Oooh, Ziggy!" they said, as they both ran off in the opposite direction.

"Sorry. They were my little brother and sister, Blue and Lola," he explained. It was obvious Ziggy had already mentioned me to his whole family.

One night at a party, Ziggy tried to kiss me. Even though I liked him a lot, I decided I was not going to risk getting hurt again, and when he asked why I would not kiss him, I told him I did not want a relationship.

"I'm going back home to the West Coast," I said.

"But why?" he asked.

"Because I have to."

I had never been in a relationship or at least one that lasted longer than three days. Often I would be attached to a guy, only to be dumped after he got what he wanted, leaving me feeling used and abused. I did not want that to happen again, so in order to protect the friendship, I lied. I did not really have to go back home because there was no one to go back to. It was just an excuse. I really liked Ziggy, but I feared losing him as a friend if it did not work out.

Two weeks after telling Ziggy I was returning home to the West Coast, I left. I felt it was the saddest day of my life when I jumped on the train and said good-bye. I really did not know what I was doing or thinking. Maybe I liked the attention and just wanted to see how much he really liked me and did not want to see me go.

As the train left the station, I had a horrible feeling that I shouldn't be leaving but ignored it, saying, "Good-bye, Ziggy," over and over to myself. I did not have enough money to go all the way, so I got off the train at the next major city. I found a place to stay while I waited for my next dole payment.

The place I stayed in was a ratty little hostel in the city centre. The only nice thing about this place was that my room had a fantastic view. During the day, the view was a grey old mess, with street bins overflowing with rubbish and the occasional used syringe lying on the ground, but at night, the city lights were pretty, making the view from my window look magical.

I got ready to check out the area, but when I tried to leave, one of the hostel workers prevented me. He had signed me in, and knowing my age, advised me that it was far too dangerous for a child my age to be wandering in that particular area. I was shocked because I had not had anyone tell me what to do since I had left home, but I took his advice and stayed in.

The next morning I was escorted to another hostel in another suburb, where I stayed for two weeks until my payday. When that day arrived, I went down town to organize my ticket, but as I prepared to buy the ticket, I had a strong feeling I should head back to the place I'd just left.

Go back ... an inner voice prompted.

I believed it was the voice of God prompting me. Even though I did not understand the reason behind the command, peace came over me as I booked the ticket back.

When I arrived, I went straight around to Ziggy's place, and his eyes lit up when he saw me walk in through the door.

"I'm back!" I yelled.

I was so happy to see him I ran up and bear hugged him, and he hugged me back. Ziggy's brother Mack was not very happy. I think he felt a little jealous, as the boys were very close, and maybe Mack feared he was losing his mate.

I admired their love for one another. The family did not have much, but they had love and it touched me because that was all I had ever wanted from my own family. I really wanted to be part of it.

Later on, this prompted me to tell their mum, Sapphire, all about myself. I wanted her to know absolutely everything, not leaving anything out. I felt it was the right thing to do, no matter how ugly the truth was. I needed to be open so they could accept me for who I truly was. I believed with all my heart that honesty was the best policy in making it work. I have to admit Sapphire was a little shocked when I told her, but later she seemed relieved and happy.

It was now several months later, and I was in love! Ziggy and I had been together for nine months. At the time, we were living with a family and had our own room downstairs.

One morning I woke up wondering about my monthly period, as it was nine and a half weeks late. I told Rena, the mother of the family we were staying with, and she told me I could be pregnant. I was so scared to hear the word pregnant. I had never wanted children. I used to say I would never bring a child into this cruel world.

Rena suggested I get a pregnancy test. When I took the test, it read positive, and I panicked. *How can this be?* I thought. *I'm still young, I'm an alcoholic, and I'm not fit or ready to be a mum.*

I had all the excuses and reasons under the sun, but I was forgetting the fact that I needed to take responsibility for my actions. I found myself sinking into a state of depression.

Then Rena's husband, Sean, overheard me talking about an abortion. He talked straight with me. "I'm an adopted child, and I'm thankful I was adopted and not aborted. Please reconsider your decision; I beg you. Don't kill your baby."

Wow! I felt even more depressed because now I felt as though I had no choice in the matter. I was going to be a mum whether I liked it or not.

I ran downstairs and threw myself on my bed face-first, with thoughts that if I hit the bed hard enough I would create a miscarriage.

I cried and cried until Rena came in to talk with me. She sat me up and dried my tears before challenging me to see what being a mum could do for me, and the benefits this little bundle could bring to my life. She helped me see that I was capable of looking after my baby. Then she took me to a place in town where they counselled me and offered assistance in caring for the baby's needs and mine. They told me if I needed help in any way, they were there for that reason.

Finally and for the first time ever, I had a reason to live. I instantly gave up drinking, for I had decided I was keeping my baby. I felt more confident about my pregnancy, and as the months progressed, I felt a little excited. I experienced joy, and it was nice.

After going to an antenatal class, seeing the ultrasound, and hearing the baby's heartbeat, the pregnancy become real to Ziggy and me. I remember thinking, *What a miracle!* Our baby was due on June 6, 1990, and we were both very excited about becoming parents. I had just turned eighteen, and it was the quietest (soberest) birthday ever.

Five months later Rena had an affair with her drug dealer, and when Sean, her husband, found out, all hell broke loose. Ziggy and I were out of there! We moved into his mum's place. I was seven months pregnant and needed somewhere stable to live.

I felt secure in their home, which they had been living in for thirteen years. While there, I made every effort to help by cooking and cleaning for the whole family. I grew to love Sapphire as if she was my own mother, and serving her came easy.

Two weeks before my due date, I was huge and sick of it. I was getting up three times a night to go to the toilet and could not sleep properly anymore. Even with the lack of sleep, I felt an excess amount of energy come over me, which prompted me to clean out my bedroom from ceiling to floor. I could not believe how much energy I had. Sapphire laughed and said I was going to have the baby soon, calling this behaviour "preparing the nest."

On June 10, 1990, I was now four days overdue and feeling totally exhausted from the pregnancy. I sat up in my bed and decided I was not going to take it anymore. "Today is the day!" I declared confidently.

It was as though I spoke it into being, because right after that I felt a very strong pain in my abdomen, which lasted a few seconds before fading away. This being my first pregnancy, I was not very sure what to expect. After experiencing that pain, I was not keen on the whole labour thing at all! I managed to get myself out of bed with great difficulty and went to Sapphire's room.

"Mum, I just got a big pain. What does that mean?" I asked.

"Have a look at the time, love, just in case you get another pain, so we can time it," she said, rolling a big three-papery joint.

I sat and talked with her over a coffee. Normally I would have had a toke on her joint, but I was not going to do it this particular morning. All of a sudden there was another pain, stronger than the first and forty minutes since the first one. I began to feel scared. I did not know what was going to happen, and I was trying to work out in my head how a baby was going to exit my body.

"I think you might be in the early stages of labour," Sapphire said. "What do you say we go for a walk across the road to Keith's house and ring the hospital?"

"Yep," I squeaked.

We rang the hospital, and after answering a series of questions, they told me to come in. Just then I got another strong pain, which was only twenty minutes from the second one. We quickly rang a taxi and went back home to gather my things. That was when I burst into tears, and with mixed emotions I asked for God's help and comfort in this amazing time of my life.

"Oh Lord, I'm scared. Help me, please," I prayed.

By the time I got to the hospital, the pains were ten minutes apart. They took me to a room and dressed me in a gown. I had severe back pain, and Ziggy helped by rubbing my back. The pain was unbearable even after the painkiller injection and application of nitrous oxide gas. I was nodding off between contractions, and before I knew it, nine hours had passed.

"How are you feeling? Has the injection worn off yet?" asked a midwife.

"Yes," I cried.

"Okay, love, we're going to do some hard work now, and then it will all be over."

"Hard work?" I cried. "It's hard work now!"

The doctor arrived and nurses wheeled in a see-through crib, which they placed under a heater. Everything was happening so fast.

"We're going to break your waters, and that should get things moving," the doctor said.

After the sound of snapping gloves, I felt a huge pool of warm water flow all over the bed. Now the pain was so unbearable that I was holding onto the bed head with all my might, pulling on the bars. This pain was unbelievable! I would not wish it on my worst enemy.

"Push!" a nurse yelled. "Good girl, that's great."

"Push again" the doctor said. "I can see the head now. One more push, love, and bubby will be out."

I gave it all my might. I just wanted it to stop. Finally, it was as if I heard a popping sound.

The midwife yelled, "It's a boy, a beautiful baby boy! Congratulations!"

I was laughing and crying at the same time, overwhelmed and exhausted. They placed him on my chest, and I found myself looking at my son! Wow! I could not believe my eyes. He was beautiful. Something happened in me when I looked at him for the very first time. We named him Baron, and he was perfect.

Ziggy and I were very much in love. People would often comment on how much they wished they could find a relationship like ours because it was very special. Having Baron totally completed our love. For once in my life I was experiencing amazing, wonderful joy.

It was early on a Monday morning. I got up to make bubby a bottle and give Blue and Lola a nudge to get up for school. Lola got up but Blue played up, not wanting to go to school anymore. Mum and Mack had to take Blue to school with the help of a local cop because Blue became hard to handle and very distressed.

One day, when Blue was turning twelve and in seventh grade, I caught him trying to roll a joint in his bedroom. From then on he began cracking up, saying he wanted to go and live with his dad, who had left when Blue was just a baby. Blue became more and more rebellious. I suggested to Sapphire that it wouldn't hurt for Blue to go, and finally she agreed. Mack offered to take Blue, which made her feel a whole lot better about the decision.

After Mack and Blue left, life became very dull. Mack was the jokester while Blue, with his red hair and temper, would keep us all on our toes. We began to miss them very much, and there was no news of when they might return.

Six months later Ziggy and I decided we'd had enough of where we were and made the decision to move to the West Coast. We saved $2,000 dealing dope. I figured if I moved back, it might prompt my family to return from Italy. I really missed them. I had not seen them in years, and I was hanging out to introduce them to their new grandson, Baron.

CHAPTER SIX

Divine Intervention

It was January 1991. While Iraq was at war in the Gulf, we were on our way back west. I was feeling rather nervous about the decision. We had one stopover where we would change aircraft, but as we waited to board the second plane, we heard our names called through the loud speakers, followed by a request to go to the nearest flight information counter.

Our first thought was that Blue and Mack had driven up to say farewell. They lived only three hours or so from the airport. When we got to flight information, the staff apologized, advising that there were no more flights going west.

"What do you mean?" I asked.

They told us that because of what was happening in Iraq, the planes were grounded over refuelling issues. They apologized for the inconvenience, adding, "We would like to assist you by flying you back to your point of departure free of charge." They then handed us complimentary vouchers for a free lunch at their café.

I could not believe it! We were shocked that we hadn't been told *before* we left. What the hell were we going to do now?

I did not want to backtrack, and besides, we had sold all our belongings, including the baby's cot. I was done with the place. We had been dealing dope for years, and I was sick of the lifestyle.

"I'm not going back, Ziggy!" I said.

"Maybe we can stay with Mack, just until the war in Iraq ends," Ziggy responded, looking through the phone book for Mack's number. This sounded very promising!

I was wondering if it was all God's idea that I could not get back home. When I thought about it, who was I going back for anyway? It was not as if my family was there; they were in Italy. The more I thought about it, the more I felt at peace about what was happening.

When I had initially been making the plans to return to my home, I had been nervous as hell wondering if I was making the right choice. It occurred to me life is full of surprises. When you think you have it all worked out, something happens—"Surprise!" All of a sudden, you have no idea at all what is happening!

Three hours later Mack arrived at the airport. He was by himself in a little green Sigma, with a trailer on the back for our bags. Mack was glad we were not flying on, and part of me was glad too.

It was dark as we drove along a dirt road. I saw a light in the distance, and finally we stopped at a big house on a hill. I was excited to see Blue standing under the porch light. He was just as excited to see us. Abby, the woman they were living with, welcomed us inside, where we sat and talked over a hot chocolate and a smoke.

I woke early the next morning to the most beautiful scenery of rolling green hills and valleys. Wow! It was breathtaking. I walked out onto the porch to catch the warmth of the sun and stepped in some chook (chicken) poop! I called Ziggy to come and have a look at the view. Baby was still asleep, so Ziggy and I were able to catch the moment together over a cuppa and a smoke. It was lovely to hear the sounds of nature instead of cars. Birds sang, chooks clucked and scratched, and cows mooed.

Abby kindly offered to let us stay for however long it took us to get ourselves our own home, but instead of adding to the crowd in the house where we'd all be in each other's faces, Ziggy and I hired a caravan, which we hooked up beside the house. Ziggy found some work with his dad picking tomatoes. On the weekend they picked capsicums on another bit of land their dad had leased.

Ziggy was able to experience a relationship with his dad again. It was really good to see them both spending quality time together. Their father had left Sapphire and the kids when Ziggy was only four. Sapphire told me it had broken Ziggy's little heart when his daddy never came home one night. Night after night he waited at the door with his favourite crocheted blanket held close to his chest, a confused look on his face saying, "Where's my daddy?"

During the time we lived there, we were able to save some money for a car, and I went for my license, which I got, after two tests—I failed the first test because of speeding!

Six months later Ziggy and I were offered a place behind his dad's house. It was a one-bedroom cottage on acreage, overlooking valleys of green with a huge dam of seemingly endless water. It was a perfect size for the three of us and very cosy. We were excited to get it.

Not long after that we bought our first car. It was an old XT Falcon. We bought it from an old couple who lived in the area. They had owned it all their lives and it was in good nick.

Everything was falling into place. We were building a life together, and it was really nice.

I felt grateful that our plans had changed because I had taken to nice, quiet country living. However, a void remained in my heart for my own family, whom I had not seen for eight years. I would often wonder about the possibility of seeing them again.

When Baron was twelve months old, Ziggy and I started planning our second baby. I thought that if I conceived at this time, there would be two years between Baron and the baby—a nice gap so they would grow up to be close to one another.

We later received news that Lola, Ziggy's sister, had fallen pregnant and because she was only fifteen, she was considering adoption. We all tried to encourage her to keep the baby, but her age made this difficult. Lola was three months further into her pregnancy than I. When our little nephew was finally born, Lola changed her mind, as we hoped she would. Mack and Blue decided to go and see baby Cruz, the new addition to the family.

Three months later I had a baby boy, whom we named Steele. He was born with the umbilical cord wrapped round his neck, and I freaked out when he was not breathing. This was yet another close call that had me turning to God.

When I look back, it all seems surreal. It was as though I had a conscious feeling that God was always there, even though I could not see Him—it was an inexplicable feeling. I believe that with every close call I experienced, my faith grew that little bit stronger. Yet I could not put my finger on what it was about this faith I was experiencing. I would often find myself thinking a lot about my past religion. I was always trying to make sense of what I was feeling and why I was feeling it.

I wanted answers, and I believe this is why I kept seeking this spiritual Being called God. I believed the more I sought God, the more He would reveal Himself through things in life that mattered most.

Our new baby's ordeal at birth caused him to have minimal damage to his brain, but nothing a little speech therapy could not fix when he started school. He had problems with his fine motor skills at first, but now he is as normal as the next person. He is, however, a bit more emotional than our other children, and I believe I treat him a little differently.

After we brought him home from hospital on 2 April 1992, we were one month into autumn, and seasonal work was slowly running out. The area we were living in was a fruit-growing area in high country. During winter, the weather would get very cold with frosts, and if you were lucky, you would sometimes see a bit of snow. The international backpackers who picked the seasonal fruit would leave by the end of autumn, around May and June. So unless you had a cosy job indoors, you could find yourself unemployed, with a choice of either hibernating for winter or moving on.

Ziggy and I made the decision to leave town in a quest to find work. A town further up the coast sounded like the way to go, with its large sugarcane farms. We also heard rumours of work in tomato fields. We headed north and found a place to stay right on a beach. We only stayed for six months because it turned out there wasn't a whole lot of work up there either. Yet those six months were enough time to settle into a routine for our new baby.

While we were there, Ziggy began to look homesick. It didn't help that he was stuck in the house with no work. I would often see him staring out the window looking sad. When I asked him what was wrong, he would not answer. I figured he was missing his family. After phoning them one day, Mack, Lola, and Blue came to visit for a few days. They brought along our little nephew, Cruz, whom we met for the first time. Ziggy seemed very happy while they were with us, but he reverted to that quiet state again when they left.

I have to admit it was very lonely during those six months. It was hard not knowing anyone. I asked Ziggy if he wanted to return home, but he would not answer me. I assured him we would go back if it was what he really wanted.

A couple of months later we moved back home, reuniting once more with his family.

I have to say it felt great to be back. After all, they were like family to me, the family I'd never had. I also noticed that Ziggy was a lot happier. We found our own place and began to settle down again.

Although I was now living a settled life, I was still open to that "anything goes" lifestyle. I smoked very little pot, but if we had a birthday party, I was the first to get drunk after the kids were all down for the night. I sold marijuana and was still open to having a shot of whizz if it ever came my way.

Quite often, when I went shopping, whether I was low on cash or not, I would find myself stealing razors and very expensive hair products, simply because I felt they were far too expensive. My attitude was, "Why should I have to pay that much?"

Every second word in my vocabulary was a swear word, except in the company of old ladies! I would often tell white lies and great big lies to accommodate myself in any situation. I also had an attitude that declared loudly that the world owed me something.

I lived life like a fool headed for disaster, but my two boys never missed out on a thing; they were both very much loved.

Only God knew what was waiting ahead for them.

My carefree lifestyle was about to take a turn for the worse.

Six months later—not long after I turned twenty-one—Mum Sapphire and Lola made plans for us girls to have a girls' night out. We did this quite often, and sometimes Grandma (Sapphire's mum) came along as well. At fifty, she was a party animal and was always keen to have a toke on a joint when it was going around.

Earlier that afternoon a fellow who scored dope regularly from us asked if we were interested in amphetamines. My eyes lit up. It had been nearly three years since I'd had any. We swapped him some dope for a bag of speed, enough to share between Ziggy, Mack, and me.

The boys eagerly watched me mix it up in the spoon. They had never seen this done before. I strapped my arm up with a belt and proceeded to have a shot. "Oh yeah, that's what I'm talking about!" I said as the initial rush hit me.

Ziggy and Mack had never had IV drugs before, let alone used a needle, so I had to do them both up. They were anxious as to what to expect. Their facial expressions could tell you what was going through their minds, and after they both had some, Mack turned into a motor mouth, while Ziggy went all quiet and reserved.

"How do you feel, babe?" I asked Ziggy.

"Yeah, all right," he replied.

I did not need to ask Mack.

"Good, I'm ready to party with the girls tonight, so I'm going to get ready," I said.

I made up some bags of dope for Ziggy to sell and hid them in the hallway cupboard under some towels. I kissed my boys good night and waited for them to drift off to sleep before heading out to meet the girls.

The night went off, and we all had a good time before cabbing it home at three in the morning. I staggered in through the front door to find Ziggy still up and waiting for me. I think I blubbered a bit and then crashed on top of my bed, shoes and all. I woke up a few hours later with a massive hangover and Mack giving me hell over it. I noticed Ziggy looked a bit off-colour.

"What did you do last night? Did you sell any weed?" I asked.

"No, someone jumped through the window and stole it," Ziggy explained.

"What?" I yelled at him. "Who?"

Ziggy was not making a lot of sense, and I was freaking out about owing my dealer all that money. I argued and yelled at Ziggy, but he just stood there staring into space.

Mack went to check for the dope, ripping my cupboard to bits but never finding it.

I harassed Ziggy all day because the story of someone jumping through the window and taking the dope did not make sense. I was angry at Ziggy because I thought he was lying and did not have enough balls to tell me he had smoked it.

That night while I was bathing the two boys, I reached into the cupboard for some towels and thought I might just check under them in the spot where I had initially hidden the dope. I had a feeling Mack might not have searched thoroughly. Bingo! There it was! I was deliriously happy.

I couldn't wait to tell Ziggy and apologize for going off at him, but then, in that moment of joy, something dawned on me. I asked myself, "Why did Ziggy say a man jumped through the window?"

My next question was, "Why did he say it if it wasn't true?"

Ziggy and Mack were out dropping off deals. When they got back, I yelled out to them, "I found it! Mack, you idiot, you said it was gone!"

That was when Mack pulled me aside and told me that while they were out, Ziggy had confided in him, telling him he felt like he was going mad.

Ziggy smoked a lot of cannabis. He was heavily addicted to it. He would go through an ounce in a week. I thought that once we had children he would slow down, but he didn't. I believe marijuana was his way of escaping painful events of earlier years.

That evening, after I had put the boys to bed, Ziggy was sitting in his chair having his nightly cones, and I was making us a cup of tea. Ziggy was sitting very quietly. Something was clearly very wrong. Ziggy had not been himself since our girls' night out.

I asked Ziggy what was wrong, apologizing again for going off on him that night. He just stared at me through glassy eyes. It was as if he couldn't speak. I hugged him tight, tears streaming down my face, and I had flashbacks of our life together. I wondered if he would ever be the same again.

As it was so hot, I grabbed a foam mattress and put it by the front door. We lay there together silently, my head on his chest. I did not know what else to do. I just wanted to hold him. I did not know who to call. I knew he was having some kind of breakdown. I thought if we could go to sleep, he would wake up in the morning and everything would be back to normal.

Just as I began to doze off, Ziggy suddenly got up, ran for the window, and jumped out. Hysterical, I ran to the window, calling out to him. I thought I was dreaming, as this sort of thing didn't normally happen. It was pitch-black outside and I couldn't see a thing. In the distance, I heard dogs barking round the neighbourhood.

"Ziggy!" I yelled.

I wanted to go after him but could not leave my boys alone. I could not call anyone as I had no phone and the nearest phone box was blocks away. I went outside and onto the road, trying to see him.

There was no sign of him. The whole episode felt eerie, demonic. *What is going on?* I thought.

I was overwhelmed with fear about calling the cops for help, just in case Ziggy had dope on him. I went back inside and lay on the mattress, convincing myself that he would soon return home. I fell asleep.

A short while later I was woken by a loud knock at the door. It was Ziggy with the cops, and my heart skipped a beat.

"Ziggy," I cried and hugged him tight.

"Good morning," one cop said. "We found him pacing around the street corner, surrounded by dogs."

The cop had a worried look on his face and asked, "Is he all right?"

"I'm not sure, but I think he's having some kind of breakdown," I explained.

Both officers suggested I take him to a doctor to get him checked out and then they left. Overwhelmed with what was happening, I cried as I got the kids ready to go over to Sapphire's place.

When I got there, only Mack and Blue were home.

"Where's Mum, Mack?" I asked.

"Why, what's wrong?" they both asked.

I explained, "There's something wrong with Ziggy. He actually jumped out the window late last night, and he hasn't spoken a word for two days straight."

Mack and Blue were at a loss for words and tried to talk to Ziggy, but he was not communicating. Next minute my dealer, Ando, drove in behind me. After chatting with Ziggy, he advised me that Ziggy was suffering from a form of mental illness and needed to go to the mental-health ward at the hospital.

"We need to let Mum know what's going on before we take him," I said.

After finding Mum, we took Ziggy to a doctor, who then referred him to the mental-health ward, where they diagnosed him as having "acute drug-induced paranoid schizophrenia."

While I waited for the prognosis, I could not help but be spooked as I watched people walking around with their eyes closed, bumping into furniture, while others were doing the unexplainable. There was one old guy dribbling from his mouth, pushing chairs around the room, and calling out to something not visibly there.

The doctor returned and told us Ziggy would need to stay in hospital for three months while they treated him. The treatment would involve a fortnightly injection of a specific drug, which would need monitoring. I signed the forms and left Ziggy there to be processed.

I went back to Mum's to talk about Ziggy's condition.

Young Blue began telling us that a particular family member had arrived on Mum's doorstep the night all us girls had gone out. When this man discovered Mum was not home, he had asked Blue for our address. He must have gone there and found Ziggy alone. (This family member was apparently responsible for some traumatic childhood experiences in Ziggy's life.)

While Blue was explaining all this, I felt sick to my stomach and could not help but wonder what had happened that night. I went looking for this individual as I wanted answers, but he was nowhere to be found, and nobody could tell me his whereabouts.

With Ziggy gone, I was not safe. I had guys hitting on me and trying to hang around all day for the dope I was selling. Seeing all of this made Mack very protective, and he would not leave my side. I was twenty-one, vulnerable, and in need of Ziggy's love, and sadly I wondered if he would ever be the man he was before he got sick.

I felt like I had lost everything. Ziggy was my world, and my whole world was falling apart. Only God knew why it was happening.

"Why is this happening? Why did you do this to me? Everyone I get close to, you take away from me!" I cried.

CHAPTER SEVEN

At Knifepoint

April 1993 and Ziggy was still in the mental-health ward. Life was challenging being a single mum, and things only got harder after receiving an eviction notice, giving us two weeks to move out.

Those two weeks slipped by fast, and I had no choice but to move all our stuff onto the veranda of a house I was still waiting approval for. Too bad if their answer was no because then I would have had to claim squatter's rights, seeing as I had nowhere else to go. Thankfully the following day the real-estate agent called, saying my application had been approved and I was good to go.

The house was a lovely, big, older style, but with Ziggy still in hospital I felt lost, scared to be in this large home on my own. I decided to ask an old friend, Blaze, to come and share it with me.

One day when I was doing some gardening, I heard someone yelling out to me from across the street. "Hey Angel, do you live here?" It was Stu, one of my best customers. He was an Indigenous guy who lived in the area.

"Yeah," I replied.

"Got any *yarndi*?" (Indigenous word for marijuana.)

"No, but I can get it. Why?"

"I want a stick. I only live around the corner. You want me to come back later?" he yelled.

"I'll chase it up and have it here by this afternoon," I replied.

I already had the dope on me to sell, but I didn't want him to know that. The reason being that if he knew, he might hang around wanting a free smoke every day—or even worse, seeing I was on my own, he might come and try to stand over me for it.

The following day Blue landed on my doorstep after a fight with Mum. I let him stay a few days until things cooled down. After all, Blaze was there, and the pair of them got on like a house on fire.

That afternoon I visited Ziggy in the hospital, and the doctors gave me the good news that Ziggy was ready for day leave. If all went well he would be ready to come home in a few weeks.

After selling that stick of dope to Stu, it wasn't long before I was dealing dope to every Indigenous fellow in town. One day two of them barged in, baling me up in the hallway of my house and threatening my life. I was very worried about what these guys were going to do, as they were well known as the "terrors" of the town. If you had something they wanted, they would take it. I felt terrified as one of them waved a knife in my face and the other pinned me against the wall by the throat as they demanded money and drugs.

Suddenly I heard a voice I recognized yelling from my back door. "*Let her go!*"

Instantly they released me and ran off out the front door. It was Cleo, an Indigenous mate from way back. "Are you okay?" she asked.

"I am now that you're here. Talk about perfect timing!"

I gave her a big hug. My friendship with Cleo went back to when I first lived in the flats with Jazz. She was there when Ziggy and I first got together, and we had stayed tight ever since. Cleo had brought along some beers, which we drank together over a good yarn and a session of yarndi.

After she left, I started worrying that the boys who tried to rob me would be back to try again.

That evening, when Blaze and Blue walked in the door, I told them what had happened, adding that I was packing up and leaving. Just then there was a blackout, and we were plunged into total darkness. I looked outside and was puzzled that my neighbour's power was still on. I scrounged around in the dark for a lighter while young Blue checked the power box to see what might have tripped the meter.

Suddenly I heard the sound of breaking glass and something heavy hitting the floor. I ducked for cover, crawling to safety as rocks were pelted through the lounge room windows. The attack stopped as suddenly as it had started. For a moment there was silence and then the sound of someone running off and dogs barking.

At first I was scared out of my wits, trying to comprehend what had just happened, but my fear quickly turned to anger and I ran out to chase after the culprits. They were gone of course. They had disappeared into the night. The only thing left to do was call the cops. I ran back home to check on my boys, and miraculously they were okay.

When the cops arrived, they took our statements and asked us some questions.

"Did you see who did this? Without an eye witness, there's not much we can do."

Blue wanted to know who it was too. I didn't want the cops to hear that it was drug-related, so I took Blue aside and whispered to him. "Don't know. That's what I was trying to explain to you before this all happened. We have to leave this house. Those fellas that threatened me today would have been behind all this. I had a feeling they'd come back after Cleo stopped them!"

Next morning I rang the real-estate agency, explaining what had happened and how I needed to break the lease. They were not happy. I frantically packed while Blue loaded the car at record speed. I organized a place to stay with our good friends Carmen and Butch, who lived at the coast. (Ziggy and I would often stay at their place on the weekends. We enjoyed spending time together over a friendly barbecue and a few drinks.)

We had already done three trips and were on our last trip to the coast. We only had fifteen kilometres to go when suddenly there was a loud bang from the engine and the car rolled to a complete stop.

I turned the key, trying to restart it, but it would not go. Blue and I looked at each other. Neither of us knew anything about cars, so we decided to lock it up and hitch the rest of the way.

After a few weeks at Carmen and Butch's place, Blue returned home and I finally got my own place in a set of units not far from the beach. There was a party atmosphere at this place, and I found myself drinking and partying quite a bit with my new neighbours.

Ziggy was allowed day leave again, only it felt strange having him around. He just wasn't the guy I knew anymore. It also did not help that I was twenty-two, young, and vulnerable and had a guy next door who was giving me a lot of attention. (I really liked this guy and he became the reason for moving twenty kilometres away to another area.)

As I was unpacking at the new house, I felt really unhappy about the way my life was going. I was sick and tired of it all. I had also been feeling sick every day for a week, and it suddenly dawned on me that I could be pregnant again. I turned to Ziggy, who was staring at me and pacing. I told him I wanted to go home, back to the West Coast. My parents had recently moved back from Italy, and I saw this as an opportunity to get Ziggy away from the dope. Ziggy was still trying to smoke pot every time his family came around, even in the state he was in. It was not helping his schizophrenia. I thought the move might help him go back to being the Ziggy I fell in love with before he got sick.

That night I told his family we were leaving. The next morning I arranged a second-hand dealer to come and buy all our stuff, and I put the money I made toward plane tickets. I rang my mum, letting her know I was expecting my third child and asked her to help us get there. Mum was thrilled with our decision and offered to pay the remainder of the fare.

We boarded the aircraft. I did not realize how heartbreaking it was going to be until we were waving Ziggy's family good-bye. It dawned on me that this was my second attempt to return to my home, only this time it felt right.

We were well into our flight when the announcement to fasten seat belts came over the loudspeakers. The pilot was preparing to land. I was a bit apprehensive, as I had not seen my own family for eight years.

We walked off the plane, and the moment arrived when I came face to face with my mum, dad, and two beautiful sisters. They were all waiting with anticipation. I cannot express how it felt to be in my family's presence. We were all hugging and kissing each other, overwhelmed and tearful with happiness.

Moving back stirred up many memories, both good and bad, with many mixed feelings that haunted me. One afternoon I thought I might take Ziggy sightseeing, so Mum let me borrow her old yellow Sigma. Something compelled me to go to the last place I saw Raven, and what happened next was something I was not expecting.

As we were sitting in the car having a smoke and looking at the park, a car stopped quite suddenly and dropped off a young woman with long, dark, curly hair. Suddenly I was fifteen again.

I yelled, "Raven!" and whistled very loudly, wanting to get this woman to turn around. When she did, I could not believe my eyes. It *was* Raven!

"Raven!" I screamed.

When she saw who I was, she yelled, "Angel!"

We ran to each other.

"Where have you been? I heard you took off."

"I did," I replied.

She grabbed me by the arm, and in a voice filled with desperation, she pleaded, "Please take me back with you."

I was shocked. After being away for five years, I could not believe Raven was still in the same place I had left her. I felt sorry for her, but the truth was, my life was not in any better shape than hers and I knew it. She invited us to sit in the park with her, while she rolled a big fat joint, just as she always did. Ziggy's eyes lit up as she lit the joint and began toking on it.

The joint went around while we happily reminisced about the times we had together, and we ended the day by exchanging phone numbers, promising to stay in touch. Sadly, I had to leave her that afternoon and go home, back to my parents' place. We said good-bye with hugs and kisses, and as we walked away, I could sense her sadness.

For three weeks, Ziggy and I had been looking around for a place of our own. Dad came home from work one day, telling us about an apartment he had seen that was up for rent. It was $75 per week fully furnished. We went to check it out and realized it was only one bedroom but had a great view of the city. Even though it was small, it was going to have to do because I wanted my own space and was sure Mum and Dad wanted theirs too. The boys had the bedroom and Ziggy and I slept on the sofa bed in the lounge room with the perfect view.

The following day Mum took me to the supermarket to get some groceries. It was raining, and as I was running for cover, I ran straight into Jade, my old friend from school.

"Jade!" I said, surprised.

"Oh my gosh, what a spinout—jinxes!" We both yelled together and laughed.

"You have to come to my place, girl; here's my phone number and address." She wrote them down, fighting the wind and rain.

That afternoon Ziggy and I went to visit Jade. She lived with her ten-year-old son in a little faded white-brick home. It was cute, cosy, and very tidy. The smell of eucalyptus filled the air. It seemed to be coming from the big gum trees surrounding the area. We made our way through to the kitchen, and her big fluffy cat scrammed from the chair on which it had been happily napping.

Jade put on the jug, and to my surprise she pulled out a bowl and a bong from the cupboard below. She began to chop up a large bud, which was already sitting in the bowl. I looked at Ziggy. His eyes, now the size of golf balls, concerned me a little, because Ziggy's love for dope was not to be taken lightly.

That afternoon, we reminisced happily about the past.

In the evening, when Ziggy and I got home, we found a card on the door of our flat, asking if I would please contact the local police station!

Oh my gosh, what does this mean? I thought.

In a flash, I remembered I'd had heaps of warrants outstanding when I'd left. Surely it could not be that. I was just a teenager at the time. Wouldn't they have wiped my record by now?

I went for a walk to the phone box and called the number on the card.

"Well, hello! Thank you for calling. You have thirteen outstanding warrants from 1988 to '89. Do you think you could come down to the station and see us?"

"Why would I need to do that? That was then, and I haven't broken the law since!" I told him. "I'm in a de facto relationship (not legally married), with two children and another baby on the way!"

"Okay. Well, we do have to deal with this one way or another," the constable replied.

I felt anxious and frustrated about the whole situation. I could not believe they would still want to punish me for my childhood mistakes. It made me realize that no matter how far we run, the choices we make have long-lasting consequences—consequences that always catch up with us.

The constable eventually talked me into coming to the station, promising me that if I came in at six that evening and stayed the night in the lockup, they would let me go early the next morning. It sounded okay, but I have to admit I was pretty scared about the whole thing. I was especially worried about leaving my boys alone with Ziggy, who really was not capable of looking after them on his own.

That evening my parents watched over the boys while I went to the lockup, where I was put in a cell. After settling in, I looked around and noticed that the place had not changed much. The yellow bars were fading, and the graffiti was still thick on the walls. An hour later, two other girls were brought into my cell. They began trying to con the cops on duty to order pizza with the money the girls had in their possession. I watched, curious to see how it would pan out.

Wishful thinking, girls, I thought, but to my surprise, the cops agreed.

No way! I had never seen this before. It just didn't happen. I began to feel as though God was making me comfortable for the night. I know it sounds silly, but I had no other explanation for it. I have to say it made my night, and the cops really did look after us. They even let us go out into the courtyard cell to smoke. While I was in the cell, I found my name still engraved in the steel doorframe—"ANGEL WOZ 'ERE '86."

The morning could not come fast enough, and I was glad when I was free again.

A week later it was payday, and I was at the supermarket doing some shopping. I was in the fresh fruit and veggie section when who should I run into but one of my old streetie friends, Coco, pushing a little toddler in a pram.

"Oh my gosh, long time no see!" I exclaimed.

My friendship with Coco went back to when we were both on the streets. Coco was bisexual and liked to hang round with the gay crowd. We used to party at the clubs where there were spectacular shows of men in drag. Drag queens were a "girl's best friend" and a lot of fun to be around.

I think I was the only heterosexual person in the clubs, with chicks hanging off me, wanting to hook up. At first I would politely decline, laughing their invitations off, saying, "Maybe in another lifetime." Later I accepted out of sheer loneliness, but I didn't travel that path for long. I wasn't comfortable with it, and something inside screamed that that kind of relationship was not for me. I also heard God's voice saying a very clear no!

After a quick catch-up, Coco and I exchanged numbers so we could keep in touch, which we did, to the extent that I was soon seeing her every day. One particular day Coco asked me if I wanted to have a "blast from the past" (meaning "let's get a shot of whizz and party like we used to"). I remembered going on speed binges with her until the supply ran dry and she began to buy heroin instead.

It had been my first time on heroin, and it had been my last. *Not my cup of tea, and I'm not sticking around for that,* I had thought at the time. It was then that I left Coco and went back to the streets. That was the last time we saw each other until now.

"So what do ya say, girl? You want to?" Coco kept asking.

"Not likely, girl! Even if I wanted to I can't, because I'm pregnant," I explained.

"It won't hurt the baby. C'mon, just this once."

Coco begged and kept on begging. I do not know how many times I declined her offer, but it was obvious she was not going to take no for an answer.

"Okay, okay, but only just this once," I replied.

Ziggy and I went off with Coco and her fiancé, with me ignoring that inner voice that was screaming, *No! Don't do it!*

Later that afternoon, as she was taking us back home, Coco told us how she had contracted hepatitis C some years before. Her fiancé looked over at her as if he did not even know about it. Fear came over me as I recalled that I had left her alone with my syringe while I went to the bathroom.

The next morning I did not feel right. I had a nagging feeling something was wrong. I rang Coco and asked if she would take me to my antenatal check up. I had a suspicious feeling that I may have contracted hepatitis C from her and asked my doctor to test me for it.

They say that there is a window period of about six months from the day of possible infection to when it will show up in your blood, but in my case, that wasn't the case. I returned to my doctor *two days later* to hear him say, "I'm sorry, but you have tested positive to the hepatitis C virus."

At the doctor's news, my heart sank with a heaviness of mixed emotions, and my mind flooded with thoughts. Coco had infected my needle—I could see no other explanation. I did not have the virus when they first tested me at the start of my pregnancy, yet now I had it.

I covered my face with my hands as a huge wave of horror crashed down on me. I felt sick to my stomach thinking about what this meant for my unborn child. All I wanted to do was curl up into a ball and die. I felt like it was the end of the world, and I wanted nothing more to do with my friend. As far as I was concerned, our friendship was over. I really let her have it as I walked out of the doctor's surgery and started my long walk back home.

I became very depressed at having contracted hepatitis C, but I eventually overcame the depression because what else could I do? What could anyone do? At the time, there was no cure.

(Hepatitis C is a blood-borne virus that is contracted by blood-to-blood contact— through shared drug-injecting equipment such as needles, blood transfusions, and tainted blood products prior to 1990. It can also be contracted through tattooing, body piercing, and other forms of skin penetration. Hepatitis is an inflammation of the liver and causes liver cirrhosis, which is where healthy cells in the liver are replaced by scar tissue, which then blocks blood flow. From what I understood, there was no cure.)

With Coco now gone, I needed my own car, but first I needed money to buy one.

I decided to start dealing dope again as money was tight and Ziggy was struggling to keep his job concreting with my dad. I did not want to rely on others anymore. I started out by buying an ounce of dope from Jade, knowing I could sell it in sticks to a guy called Vic who lived downstairs in the apartment block.

Vic was an alcoholic and would often sit and drink at the tavern across the road where there were many customers for dope. Vic would sell out in less than an hour, and I would have to buy more. I profited $2,000 in a very short time.

I decided to open a separate savings account where I could keep the money safe. Occasionally, if I had to, I would withdraw small amounts like $20 in order to purchase milk and bread.

One particular morning the balance showed that $1,000 was missing from my account. I made enquiries and found that the money had been taken out of the account at eleven the previous night, which meant it had happened while I was asleep. I later found out that it had been taken by my loving Ziggy, who had now developed a habit with speed because of hanging around with my now ex-friend and her boyfriend. I was furious.

Before Ziggy could take any more of our money, I asked Vic if he would help us bid for a car at an auction somewhere. I bought a green Sigma station wagon for $600. It smoked a little but got us from A to B, and all I needed now was to get out of the flat.

My baby was due in fewer than three weeks, and the flat was not big enough for all of us. After a week of house hunting, I found a nice little three-bedroom brick home in the next suburb not far from my old mate Jade. Two weeks later I gave birth to a healthy and beautiful baby girl, whom I named Carina, after my grandmother who lives in Italy.

"She's going to wear pink; no tomboys in this family!" I said.

I asked my doctor about the possibility of my baby contracting hepatitis C from me. I thought, *Surely if I have it, baby will catch it too.*

The doctor advised me that it was rare for a mother to transmit it to baby because the baby has its own blood supply. He added that even if I did pass it on to the baby, they would not be able to treat her until she became an adult. All they could do at this stage was give her a hepatitis B shot to help boost her immune system. I was so relieved to hear she probably didn't have it.

By this time I had learned to live with my disease in the hope that maybe one day they would find a cure for it. I became open about my disease and was not afraid of being discriminated against. I felt it was better to let people know so they were aware and felt safer by knowing about it. It also made me feel better, and I was able to cope with it more easily, knowing I did not have a great big secret inside me.

After moving away from the flats, I could no longer sell dope, as Vic was the main man with all the clientele. This meant we now had to pay for Ziggy's dope habit. It was not cheap because Ziggy was back to smoking an ounce a week. Eventually I got to know more people, and Jade put me on to her dealer, Daton, who later introduced me to their main dealer, Gina, who recognized me from high school.

Gina was Italian and one year older than I was. She was dealing in all sorts of drugs and stolen merchandise. I could not believe this sweet innocent Italian girl had gone from hairdresser to drug dealer.

One day Ziggy was hanging out for a smoke, so I went to see Gina for some tick until payday. We were doing it tough financially and Gina knew it. That was when she pulled out what looked like an eight-ball of speed (three and a half grams).

"Here, why don't you take this for $500—you can make a really good profit."

"Na, if I get caught with that stuff, I'll lose my kids for sure," I replied.

I had not touched speed since that last shot with my streetie friend, and I was not about to start, especially after contracting hepatitis C. I told Gina about Ziggy's dope habit, explaining that some dope was all I wanted from her.

Over time I noticed Ziggy and my best mate, Jade, becoming very close friends. So close that one day I accidentally found Ziggy at her place when he was supposed to be at work. He answered my knock with only his jeans on. Shocked, I quickly about-faced and walked away feeling heartbroken and devastated. It was obvious something was going on between them.

As angry as I was, I did not want to blame it on Jade. As far as I was concerned, Ziggy was the one in the wrong, as he was at her house. I wanted to end our relationship right then and there but I couldn't; my heart was anchored.

I did not know what to do. I kept thinking about my kids and how hurt they would feel if I left their father. I didn't want to see them in pain, but they suffered anyway on many nights when Ziggy would start arguments with me just so he could take off down to the local pub. I followed him one night and found him watching strippers and having a blast. I was heartbroken. If looks could kill, Ziggy would have died instantly.

I was filled with deep feelings of betrayal at his deceit and for the way he was treating me. It was as if he did not care about us anymore. We were slowly drifting apart.

Days later, I learned I was pregnant again through contraception failure. I was devastated as it was so soon after having Carina. I did not know what to do. All I knew was that I was not ready to have another baby, especially now that Ziggy was not being supportive. That was when I made a rash decision to terminate the pregnancy.

Without thinking about the decision too much, I quickly rang Gina for help, and the next day I found myself in the abortion clinic, alone and without hope. I did not want to do this but felt unable to cope.

Ziggy was somewhat saddened by the whole ordeal, but he never once tried to stop me. I do not think he even cared, otherwise he would have stayed and supported me in the clinic. Instead, he was outside with Gina doing God knows what. I suspected foul play.

I was over Ziggy's lack of consideration. When I realized there was nothing I could do to vent my anger, it quickly turned into depression. I was intensely sad and overwhelmed with feelings of regret and confusion. I hated myself and I hated Ziggy. My heart was broken, and I carried guilt around like a wheelbarrow full of wet cement. I believed that for me to stay on top of the feelings, I would need to bury them deep down in my soul. There was a fear that one day they would surface and I would have to deal with them, but at this stage, I just wanted to forget. I convinced myself the abortion never happened.

After months of enduring Ziggy's binge drinking and running amuck every night, I telephoned his family, hoping his mum or Mack could talk some sense into him. Ziggy was coming home every night drunk and abusing me. I had accused him of having an affair with one of Gina's mates who was selling dope for her, and Ziggy later confessed it was true, which cut me like a knife. I lashed out in a rage of anger and hit Ziggy over the head with a broomstick.

The following day Mack phoned asking Ziggy if he wanted to go back home for a holiday. I could not believe they were asking him to do that. I was offended that they would ask him to go away from his family, and I gave Mack a piece of my mind. In reply, he offered to pay for all of us to fly back east.

Mack had a plan to get rich quick by growing a big marijuana plantation. He said we could make $20,000 each, to start a new life. He thought money was the answer to all our problems. It sounded like a plan, but first I had to convince my own mum. You know the old saying, "Mums know everything!" I told her we were asked to go back east in order to help Ziggy's dad on a capsicum farm, which would benefit us financially—but I do not think she bought it. She seemed very annoyed by my decision to go back. I gave the real estate agency notice, and we moved back into my parents' place to wait for our departure date.

The next morning I woke up at about five o'clock and noticed Ziggy was not in bed. I went looking around the house but no Ziggy. I could not work out where he would have gone or even why. I asked Mum if I could borrow her car to see if I could find him. I had a feeling to go back to our old house, and that was where I found Ziggy, asleep on a lounge in the garage with a flagon of my dad's red wine half-full beside him.

"Ziggy!" I yelled. "What the hell are you doing here?"

He looked a mess, and I was dumbfounded as to why he would come back here. I helped him back to the car and drove back to Mum's.

The following day, Ziggy and I were showering and getting ready as we were due to fly out that night at eleven. I explained that he would have to keep an eye on things when we got back. I was worried that with Ziggy looking as though he was relapsing, his brothers would hit on me again. I had encountered problems with them being a little sleazy toward me when Ziggy got sick the first time. Young Blue had been infatuated with me, and Mack would try to get fresh. I often had to remind them that I was with Ziggy, their brother.

Departure day arrived. We finished sharing a meal with my whole family at the airport, and then it was time for us to board. We hugged each other tight, promising to keep in touch. Tears streamed down our faces, and I felt my mother's heart breaking as I walked away from her embrace with baby Carina on my hip. I felt guilty for leaving them all again and continuously waved good-bye as we walked toward our plane. I was glad to get on.

Once more my life was flying into the unknown.

It felt weird to be going back again to the very place I had run from. I looked over at Ziggy, who was looking rather anxious and getting up to go to the toilet. Right after he returned, a very gorgeous and angry hostess politely warned Ziggy that we would get a huge $5,000 fine if he smoked in the toilet again.

"What the!" I was extremely angry and thought, *How stupid of him.*

Ziggy was sweating and looked pale. The thought of him relapsing made me feel insecure, not to mention alone and unsure of my future.

CHAPTER EIGHT

Big Plans

We arrived back after a terrifying ride in a very small plane. (After we had been flying for some hours, the plane had suddenly hit heavy turbulence. We must have flown into a large air pocket. For about two seconds it had felt as though the plane was falling. All of us yelled as the wind was pushed out of our bellies. It was scary and for a split second, my life flashed before my eyes. Then it was smooth sailing all the way to the airport.)

When we landed, we found Mack waiting for us. Mack hugged Ziggy and asked him how he was feeling.

"Okay," was all Ziggy said.

We loaded the car and drove to the outskirts of town where we turned off on to a red, dusty road. The sweet smell of spring was in the air, and colourful wildflowers blossomed among thick green shrubbery as we approached a large, high-set home surrounded by banana and mango trees. The rest of the family was living there. They were all still together and it was good to see them again.

Little Cruz was now four, and Lola was raising him on her own. Blue had grown taller, and Mum had not aged a bit. She was still as stunning as ever.

We sat down around the old table with a hot cuppa and talked over a huge session of bud, while the kids played happily around the garden with Cruz, their long-lost cousin. It was just like old times, except the kids were bigger and we were all just that little bit more grown up. At least we thought so. None of the family said much about Ziggy's strange behaviour. I think they were used to him acting strange and figured it was the result of his breakdown.

Within days of being there, I noticed Mack was selling large amounts of dope, and he and Blue were constantly fighting over the bathroom at the end of the dining room. One night I was sitting at the dining table feeding Carina when Blue burst in and started squabbling with Mack from outside the bathroom door, telling Mack to let him in. I soon realized that going by the number of times this was happening each day, Mack must have been doing drugs—but which ones? I decided the next time it happened I was going to follow Mack into the bathroom. Sure enough, I found him mixing up a taste of speed. The minute I saw it I demanded he give me some. Mack looked at me in shock, but it was exactly what I needed at that point.

One night, lying in bed, unable to sleep, I got up to get a drink and use the bathroom. I was in the bathroom when I heard footsteps coming up the stairs leading to the back door. Whoever it was entered the house and headed straight for the bathroom, where I was locked in.

"Who's in there?" I heard a voice whisper.

My heart skipped a beat, and then I realized it was Mack up to his old tricks. I opened the door and he flashed a bag in my face, offering me a taste of speed. I could not resist.

After we'd had it, we stayed up all night smoking dope and talking as you do when you're high. At some point we got onto the subject of Ziggy, speaking about how things had been while we were away. That was when I told Mack how I'd thought about leaving Ziggy, after he admitted cheating on me. I explained that my mum would forever talk me out of it, using Ziggy's illness as the reason I shouldn't leave.

"I can't cope with all Ziggy's problems anymore," I said.

Mack just looked at me. I thought he might get angry, but then his mobile phone started ringing. It was a customer wanting a bag of dope. He asked if I wanted to come for a quick drive up the road and back to deliver it.

The following day Mack took us out to the property he had rented for growing a marijuana crop. It was a deserted spot in the middle of nowhere, with a spring-fed creek running through it, and a beat-up old caravan for an abode. I did not know which was safer, the caravan or the annex. There were massive holes in the caravan where any living creature could crawl in at any time, day or night.

I was disappointed Mack's intention was for us to live in such poor conditions just so we could keep an eye on a dope crop. The plants were already three feet tall, some taller. In the end, Ziggy, the kids, young Blue, and I were all dropped off at the caravan while Mack returned home to sell the dope.

After putting the kids to bed that night, Ziggy lost the plot and took off into the forest. At first I thought he had gone off for more firewood, but hours later he had not returned. I asked Blue to go look for him. I knew right then and there that this was not going to work out.

I was so glad Blue was with us or I would have freaked out. I could not sleep. Ziggy was somewhere in the bush. As soon as daybreak came, I sent Blue to look for Ziggy.

By now I was all spooked out and wanted out of this place. I started to hitchhike back to town with the kids. We were about twenty kilometres out on a back road. After walking for forty minutes, I came across a funny-looking lunch bar, which looked like a tree house. I walked up the stairs and found a phone. I had no money so I reversed the charges back to Mack, telling him to come get us. In the meantime, I kept walking in the direction of town. It was not long before I heard a car coming. Mack arrived and drove us back home.

Mack was not happy about it, but I was not going to stay on that property with no electricity, car, or phone. It was not a safe place for the kids. Mack agreed with me on that point, so after dropping me at home, he went and checked on Blue and Ziggy.

(Mack was caring and attentive to our needs. He helped with the kids, especially Carina, who was only eight and a half months old at the time.)

I now realized I was deeply attracted to Mack. That night, after I had gone to bed, I heard someone creep into my room, and as if expected, Mack climbed into my bed.

"Don't resist me," he whispered. In that moment, I gave in to his passion for me, surrendering to a seven-year resistance with a passionate kiss. There is no need to share the rest.

The next morning I kicked myself. *What am I going to do now? This is a mess,* I thought. I had begun to feel something strong for Mack and wished I had never given in. I felt almost cheated. Then I heard Mack's phone ringing. It was Blue and Ziggy wanting to come home because Ziggy was not well. Mack went to get them.

Once they returned we all went under the house. While we were sitting around the table having a cuppa, I put my hand on Ziggy's shoulder, asking how he was feeling. He went berserk. I quickly picked Carina up, out of harm's way.

Ziggy grabbed a nearby shovel, and at shoulder height, he angrily stabbed the shovel blade at me. I totally freaked out because if he had stabbed a little closer and harder, he could have decapitated both Carina and me. I could not blame him. I had been unfaithful. It was as if he knew and sensed something had happened between Mack and me.

Ziggy dropped the shovel. "You can have her, Mack. At least I'll see my kids," he cried as he ran up the stairs.

I immediately ran up behind him, screaming and asking why he had said that. I felt my heart malfunction, skipping a beat. I was torn between the brothers and could not choose. I did not know what I wanted, and the drugs were probably adding to the confusion. I knew the moment Ziggy said, "You can have her," Mack felt he had the green light to take over.

Ziggy went and locked himself in the room and would not let me in. I was now drowning in confusion because deep down in my heart I did not really want to be with either of them. I was now sure that it was only a matter of time before Ziggy and I would go our separate ways.

Days on, Ziggy was very hostile toward me, yet at the same time he acted as though nothing had happened. Every time I looked at him, I felt riddled with guilt. I began asking Mack for more speed to make myself feel better, but it only added to the awkwardness that was round everyone in the house. I wanted to leave and take my kids to a hostel, but deep down I knew that if I started walking, Mack would stop me. I felt trapped and had no choice but to stay and wallow in my mess.

Then Lola announced that she had had enough and was moving out. The family was falling apart, and I felt responsible for all of it.

The next day, when Mack, Blue, and Ziggy returned from uprooting the plants, there was a letter waiting for Mack—an eviction notice. He had two weeks to move out. I'd thought things could not get any worse. Mack reacted by running down to the nearest real estate and finding another house, as we had about one hundred plants with no home to call their own. We left before the two weeks were up, Mack hiring a huge truck so we could transport our stuff and the plants to the new property.

We worked hard to prepare the soil and dig the holes for replanting. The sudden move had stressed the plants, and most of them started to bud earlier than expected. The house we'd moved into was on one hundred and forty acres and was thirty kilometres outside town. It was an old milking farm. Looking around the sheds, I could picture the establishment when it was in full swing. All that remains today are the faded whitewashed walls of an empty shed, which is home to wild animals like the friendly giant carpet snake that quietly rests entwined along the top beam of the roof.

Although Ziggy had said what he said, we still managed to stay together. He never said any more about the day he "gave me away."

Though I knew things were not the best between us, I could not let him go. He was my soul mate! However, I kept forgetting that he'd had a nervous breakdown and was not the person he was when we'd first met. We were two very different people with two completely different stories to tell. As I pondered our future, it broke my heart to think we were eventually destined to break up.

Trying to hold onto Ziggy was only making things worse between us, so after a time, he moved out. He moved in with his sister, Lola, who was living in town with Blue. After Ziggy moved out, Mum also decided she could not stay in the same house with Mack and me pretending nothing was happening. She moved back to town with Lola, Ziggy, and Blue.

Now Mack and I had the problem of watering all the plants by ourselves. That involved carrying big drums of water on a wheelbarrow out into the paddock. It was hard work for just the two of us, but it had to be done. Things only got worse, such as when Mack's car was caught in a flash flood and half the crop was washed out during a torrential rain.

Being thirty kilometres outside town with no transport was risky, so Mack uprooted a plant and swapped it for a few grams of speed and an old 125cc Honda scooter. It was a real sight to see Mack riding that bike, but it was going to have to do until we put another motor in the XE.

As months went by, we were living on speed. In the end, it was all Mack cared about. It was also all I cared about because it was all I had besides the kids, who did not seem to have a care in the world after Uncle Mack bought them brand new bikes with the profits made from drugs.

I had no friends and no visitors apart from some members of a religious group who would come all the way out to have a "Bible study" with me. They proclaimed the end of this evil system and the establishment of a new one. With that proclamation, I wished it would all end sooner than later. It definitely would have saved me a lot of heartache to come.

The members of this religious group seemed to have a way of sparking a spiritual fire in my soul when they shared their beliefs, but their teaching never hit home with me. I guess it only made me feel worse because of the mess I was in. This would depress me, and after they left, I would wipe myself out on alcohol, only to be woken by the blaring TV—a famous speaker preaching a message of hope. I would hear, "Wake up! God loves you. Why don't you come to Him today?"

Each day I stood watching Mack pull up plants one by one to feed our addiction. I wondered what would happen once they were all gone. I began to ask myself, *What am I doing here?* I became angry with Mack. I could not believe I had let him talk me into doing this! That was when I decided enough was enough. I would grow my own crop, sell it, and move back to the West Coast.

The climate where we were living was perfect for growing dope fast, but I had to hurry because winter was only months away. The following morning at dawn I went down the back to dig the holes for the plants. Then I selected ten of the best seedlings in their pots and planted them. These were mine, and they were going to get me home.

Six weeks later, they had grown six feet tall. Winter was fast approaching, and with the cooler weather, the plants started to bud. Mack was down to only a few plants and already eyeing mine off.

Money was now very scarce, and we had to rely fully on our dole payments to support our drug habits. We fell behind in the rent, which resulted in an eviction notice. We had no transport, and we knew we had to get the car fixed. The motor was sitting there, and we were the only ones to fix it. We spent endless nights on speed and replacing the motor in Mack's car. We had to keep working all night and well into the next morning. Finally it was finished. With our fingers crossed, Mack attempted to start it. We could not believe it when the engine roared to life. It was exciting that something was finally going right. Just in time too, because the real estate was coming sometime that day. We didn't want to be there when they arrived.

We began loading the car with all that we could fit, leaving just enough room in the boot to shove in my dope plants. We did not intend to return to get anything else because the real-estate agency was coming to seize our belongings for the rent arrears. We left the place in a mess and headed straight for another little town in search of a place to stay.

As we were driving to a real-estate agent, we spotted a little house along a creek with a private sign that said FOR RENT. The house was a small two-bedroom cottage. We had a better chance of renting that than going through a real-estate agency, where we would have been blacklisted. We phoned about the cottage and got it straight away. We managed to squeeze into it and made plans to find something bigger when we could. It was cute and peaceful, but it was not long before the cops came looking for us over a marijuana plant I had left growing on the other property. I was charged with possession and cultivation of a dangerous drug.

A few weeks later we found a private two-bedroom house on a hill where we could all spread out a bit. It was here that I reached a critical point in my life. I remember asking myself, "Is this all there is? This can't be it!" I began looking for greener grass over the fence and decided there was no reason to stay there since Mum Sapphire, Lola, Blue, and Ziggy had all moved away and our plans to get rich on a marijuana crop had failed big time!

We were broke all over again. We had smoked all my dope, the dope that was to have gotten me back west. Now what were we to do? We were back to square one. I felt I had to do something about it, but the big question was, how was I going to raise the money we'd need?

Without going into too much detail, I placed an ad in a local newspaper. My intention was to meet a rich old "sugar daddy," someone who would listen to my sad, desperate life story and jump at the chance to rescue me. Prostitution was no stranger to me.

I was looking for a lonely, much older man who wanted company more than anything else. The calls came in and after rejecting many of them, I finally found my man. He was a sixty-five-year-old who told me he was a public figure in the community and was looking for company. After meeting up with him and sharing my reasons for what I was doing, he offered to pay our plane fares if I would stay the entire night with him. The following morning he took me to the travel agent and paid for our tickets back west.

Now that the tickets were finally booked, I was left with the question: What was I going to tell my mother about my situation with Ziggy and Mack?

My life revolved around telling lies, and I even began believing them.

Shortly after arriving back home on the West Coast, I told my family some crazy story that Ziggy was ill and would stay with his mother until he got better. I also added that Mack, who worked at a meat works, had come to look after us and find a job at one of the meat works there. (At least that part was true. Mack *was* a slaughter man, and a good one at that.) My parents seemed comfortable with the story I gave them, and Mum went off to make a bed for Mack in the lounge while I made beds for me and the kids in my sister's bedroom.

The following day I left the kids with Mum and went to visit my old drug dealer, Gina. I wanted to show Mack how much better the quality of the speed was compared to the speed in his home back east. Gina was surprised to see me but shocked to hear me ask for the speed. She grinned and threw a packet of speed and some picks on the table in front of me. Mack and I went halves, and it was the best feeling I'd had for a long time. Gina asked about Ziggy, and I told her the same story I had told my folks, except I do not think she bought it for a moment.

After six weeks, we found our own place. It was a nice cosy three-bedroom brick home with lots of shrubs all around and a fenced-in backyard for privacy.

One day Gina asked me to babysit for her. She had a little girl who was always gorgeously dressed in pink. When she returned, she asked me for a huge favour. She said she needed to go out of town for the night and wanted me to hold some heroin and speed deals for some folks who were going to collect it. I freaked out, shocked!

"Heroin—do you use that stuff?" I asked.

"No, silly, I just sell it and make a profit because there's a huge demand for it."

Nevertheless, I felt very scared about selling hard drugs, and I hummed and hawed about it. I was already feeling bad about using them, never mind selling them. The thought of being busted and losing my kids frightened the hell out of me. Still, she insisted, assuring me it would be okay. It was only one night, and she promised to reward me greatly for it. I agreed to do it and discovered that it was not that bad. When she got back, she looked after me with a nice wad of cash and a bag of *coota* (highest quality) speed for my personal use.

A few days later Gina asked if I would do the same again. I wanted to know why she could not get her other dealers to do it. She said they could not be trusted as they were all heroin users—I was not. I felt obligated, believing I had no choice. I was afraid that if I didn't do it, she wouldn't look after me anymore, so I gave in and agreed to do it one more time. The next day she dropped the stuff in my lap and took off again.

Gina was making trips interstate, picking up the coota and bringing it back. I made $2,000 just helping her move the gear, and with that money, we bought ourselves our first car.

The phone rang.

"The phone, someone get the phone!" Mack yelled from the toilet.

I answered it, thinking it was just another customer, but instead it was Ziggy, announcing he was coming for a visit to see the kids. He told me he would be arriving the following week. I did not really want him to come, but as awkward as it was, I could not really stop him. He was the father of my three children and had every right to see them.

The next day at about six in the morning, someone was knocking. It was Gina, wearing her ever-so-gorgeous Italian smile. She walked in and sat at the kitchen table. I put the jug on while she unpacked her money and drugs all over my kitchen table.

"I've been awake all night. Do you want a shot?" She opened up an ounce bag of speed.

"Do I ever!" I replied, pouring a cup of boiled water.

I handed her a clean spoon, and she put in enough speed for three or four people. I drew up water in the syringe and started mixing the shot.

I was getting my arm ready to inject when Gina spoke. "I need you to sell this and watch bubs (baby) for me again."

She handed over two clip-top bags of what looked like speed and heroin.

I continued to inject myself, knowing this shot was coming at a high price. I just nodded. A few months had passed since I first started selling for Gina, and I was getting familiar with all of her customers, except for one.

The phone was ringing hot when I heard a knock. When I opened the door, I was shocked to find a seven-foot Indigenous bloke standing on the other side of my security screen.

"Hi, my name is Jack. I'm a friend of Gina's. I want to score a gram of *goee*, sis, if that's all right."

For a split second I found myself going back to the night when Spider attacked me. The memory was still very fresh in my mind. I contemplated my answer, as I knew the only thing keeping me safe was the flimsy security screen between us. I asked God for protection, knowing that if this guy really wanted to hurt me, that security door was no match for him. I took a deep breath, put on a mask of courage, and unlocked the screen door.

Mack went and fetched the gram while I stayed with Jack and talked. He mentioned that he knew of me, as Spider was his first cousin. He went on to say it was all in the past, but as he talked, I was getting pretty worked up.

Mack walked in with the gram just in time to change the subject. Mack handed him the bag. Jack tasted it and then got up to leave.

"I don't get paid until tomorrow, but I have some collateral in the car you can have until I do," he said, and he went off to get it.

We really had no say in the matter as this huge black man could easily have robbed us. Collateral sounded good. He returned holding something in a pillowcase. Then he began to pull out what looked like a gun, in pieces. My heart started pounding at a hundred miles per hour as he began joining the pieces together. The sound of metal hitting metal was terrifying. The fear that he could use this weapon to rob us overwhelmed me. He then handed me two bullets.

"Look after this baby for me until I get paid." He left.

As we put the shotgun away, the phone rang. It was Ziggy asking if we could pick him up from the bus depot as he had just arrived in town. This was not a good time for family reunions. Ziggy had no idea what we were up to. However, he was about to find out, because soon after returning home with him, the phone started ringing hot.

While Mack was out seeing to the needs of the callers, I was using the bathroom. I heard a racket at the front door and ran to see what all the noise was. To my surprise, I saw a plain-clothes detective with a crowbar in both hands trying to rip the door off its hinges while Ziggy was trying to unlock it. The detective saw me standing behind Ziggy.

"Stay where you are and put your hands on your head," he yelled.

In that split second I desperately wanted to stash the drugs that were on me, but before I knew it, I was rushed by detectives to a separate room where a female officer searched me and found in my possession the clip-top bag containing heroin weighing 4.5 grams and a bag of amphetamines that weighed just under an ounce. I was busted and now had to think fast. (Heroin was regarded as the gutter drug, causing death and destruction to humanity and woe to anyone selling it.)

While they were dealing with me, I came up with an idea to cry "addict," as this way I would get off lighter if the judge knew I was selling it to support my habit. Through the front window I saw Mack. The cops had him detained until they were ready to take us to the police station.

Once we got there, they interrogated us for eight hours, later charging us with a series of charges, which included conspiracy to sell and supply, possession of heroin with intent to sell and supply, possession of amphetamines with intent to sell and supply, and possession of a firearm and ammunition (x2).

These were all very serious charges and I did not think we would be getting out on bail, but thankfully the detectives were happy to give us personal bail with an ISO (intense supervision order). This meant we had to report to the main police station three times a week until our court date. As Mack and I walked out of the police station, we embraced each other. I cried, knowing how close we had been to not getting out at all. After this I became very depressed knowing that, once trialled, I could go to jail and lose my children. My fear of this happening was becoming a reality.

One morning I was lying in my bed of depression and feeling hopeless. I could not stop thinking about my court date, which was fast approaching. I was miserable, and that was when I reached down the side of my waterbed and pulled out two tightly wrapped balls—one of heroin and the other speed. It was no surprise to me that I would continue dealing with drugs.

I looked at the ball of heroin and said to myself, "What the hell. I'm feeling as low as the stuff itself." I placed a small rock of heroin, the size of a grain of rice, onto a piece of foil and began to smoke it through a rolled up fifty dollar bill, just as I had seen my customers do. (This technique is called chasing the dragon.) I thought taking the drug this way was not as bad as injecting it, but I was completely deceived.

On the fourth day I felt I was over my depression and decided I did not need the drug anymore. However, that night after climbing into bed, I could not get comfortable. I was overwhelmed with feelings of anxiety and had hot and cold flashes. I tossed, turned, and started to wonder if the discomfort was due to the heroin I had been smoking for the last three days. Now I was curious to see what would happen if I smoked a little more. Immediately after the first toke, I felt a rush of relief that travelled from my feet up to my brain, and the discomfort was completely gone.

The next day I told Mack I had become a little hooked on heroin. He admitted that he was also having a smoke here and there. We could have stopped at this point, but for some reason we continued to smoke, thinking at the time it was the answer to all our worries.

The following day I was going about my daily chores when I decided to have a smoke. I pulled a bag of heroin out of my pocket—and it was just as well I did because all of a sudden a band of undercover cops came rushing through the front door. They were hoping to catch me red-handed again.

I quickly picked up the dirty wash that was lying at my feet and walked out of the bathroom, pretending I never saw them. They ordered me to stop, drop the wash, and put my hands on my head. As I let go of the laundry I let go of the drugs too and prayed they would not search the pile. A female officer grabbed me and frisked me while the other picked up a pair of jeans from the pile of washing. She tossed them back after examining them.

After searching me and finding nothing, the female officer seemed happy that the search was complete. She said to the other officer, "She's right, she's got nothing," and they left.

That was close, as another charge would have breached my orders and sent me racing to jail. With the cops raiding our home twice in one month, the landlords, who lived right next door, decided to hand us an eviction notice.

Days later I was packing and waiting to hear back about another house just up the road. It was a beaten-up old house, but it was our last resort, and I was desperate and fearful that I would not have a home for my children before I was due to face court. I managed to befriend the landlord, using my Italian heritage, as she was Italian too. Later that afternoon she rang me with a yes, and I immediately started the moving process. My mum rocked up to help, but when she saw the house she freaked out, saying it was an unstable death trap. I have to admit that yes, it was pretty bad, but we were fortunate to have it.

One week later, on 27 February 1998, court was in session and Mack and I were at the mercy of the magistrate. After entering the guilty plea, there was a long pause, and I felt sweat beads forming on my forehead.

Then the magistrate of the district court spoke, looking up at us through his tiny glasses. He ordered that an extension of twelve months be added to our ISO (intensive supervision order).

Did I hear correctly? I was shocked, as I had been expecting at least three months' jail. The magistrate explained that we had completed the ISO with no defaults and it was only fair to give us a chance, bearing in mind that if we failed to comply with the order, we would automatically be in breach and would be sent back to court for re-sentencing.

I was very relieved but I was also very worried, worried about being able to meet those demands. What if we forgot to sign in or got booked for speeding? What if we had an accident in our rush to be on time? That would be even worse. Twelve months was a long time for such an intense order—and there was more. I was to do 240 hours of community work and pass a series of drug tests, which meant I had to wear a patch on my skin. This patch would be tested for drugs at my next probationary appointment.

The consequences were heavy, but I was grateful I wasn't being sent to jail. It meant I could go home to my children, who were with my mother and eagerly awaiting the news. I owed it all to God. I believed with all my heart that He caused the judge to look on me with favour. My faith was in a God who really does exist and who was watching over my entire family and me.

CHAPTER NINE

Doings and Dealings

Life in our new place seemed more relaxed after my dealer went dry and I stopped dealing. I began my mission to complete the 240 hours of community work at a charity shop, where I worked three days a week while my two boys were at school and my baby girl went to day care. Mack managed to find work in a steel fabrication factory, and it was not bad pay.

Early one morning after Mack left for work, I was outside watering my garden when I heard the sound of someone running. I looked up and saw four cops running toward me. My heart skipped a beat. For a second I had to think whether I had any drugs on me. Luckily we had smoked the last of it just before Mack left for work. This was the second raid since the big bust. It seemed the cops were keen on locking me up.

That afternoon I got a visit from my youngest sister Gianna, who was planning to take her third sacrament in the Catholic faith. This sacrament was confirmation: sacrament of the spirit. (There are seven sacraments in the Catholic faith.) My mother encouraged me to do it with my sister as we had already received the first two, baptism and holy communion.

First we both had to commit ourselves to a four-week study in preparation to receive the sacrament. It all sounded good and I agreed to do it, as God was already very real in my life. I also felt it might make my mother proud of me after I had disappointed her for so long.

Only days before I was to receive my sacrament, I had to go to the priest and confess all the sins I had committed since my last confession, which was when I received my holy communion sacrament seventeen years previously. A lot had happened since then, and I was worried that the priest would have a heart attack after hearing my confessions. Luckily for him I left out the part about being addicted to heroin as my sister was beside me, and I did not want her to know about it.

The special day finally came when the priest laid hands on my head and asked God the Holy Spirit to fill me with spiritual gifts. With the holy oil he made the sign of the cross on my forehead as he blessed me. It truly was a special day, and I did feel spiritually blessed as I walked away confirmed in the name of Mary Magdalene, with my sister Alessia on my right, ordained to be my godmother. Hmm. There was something not right about that part, but I did not let it ruin the day. I walked away from that big cathedral, feeling full of God's Spirit and ready to celebrate. Mum had a feast prepared, the likes of which you have never seen.

Ziggy had been living with us for some time now, and thanks to us he had developed a raging heroin habit. Money was scarce and our tolerance was escalating—meaning we were in need of more and more heroin each day. Ziggy decided to steal expensive name-brand clothing from big stores. The dealers loved the clothing and colognes, and they would exchange them for anything you wanted. Mack offered to be the driver while Ziggy went in to shoplift.

This went on for a few weeks, until one day Mack and Ziggy nearly ran down a security guard when he tried to stop them from getting away with a carload of stuff worth thousands of dollars. They later hid the car and reported it stolen. This episode stopped them in their tracks, so with no means to support our habits, Ziggy had no choice but to head back home while Mack and I were forced to go on the methadone program.

Methadone seemed like a dead-end street. If I was ever going to beat my heroin addiction, I would first have to overcome the methadone habit, which was harder to get off than heroin.

We were on it for two long years, during which time I was waiting for my criminal compensation payout. I knew it was getting closer. and my lawyer advised me it could arrive anytime. I was thinking that with that kind of money I could beat the methadone habit and get out of the shabby house that was still standing only by the grace of God.

On 29 December 1999, I received a check in the mail for $20,000. The first thing I did was ring my dealer for an ounce of heroin worth $12,000 in the hope of selling and buying again. We immediately packed house and bolted, owing hundreds of dollars in rent. I had the money to pay the rent but refused, due to the landlord always snooping around, breaking all the tenancy rules. I hired a ute (utility vehicle) to move our things into a two-bedroom motel room.

Finally I was free to supply myself with all the heroin I wanted. However, unless I found some customers, the supply would soon run out. That is when we decided to send a young couple into the city to hang out, spreading the word that we had good quality *gear* for sale. They did this for some days, and in exchange I paid them with smack.

Things started getting desperate. I thought if the phone did not start ringing pretty soon we would end up using the lot ourselves. However, just as we got down to our last gram, the phone started ringing non-stop. It rang the entire day long, and the next thing we knew we were ringing our dealer for another ounce.

We stayed at the motel for two months, all the while looking for a house to rent. Mack finally found one just up the road for $140 a week. It was a nice large home, but as we started packing, there was a knock at the door. A woman introduced herself, stating that she worked for the government social services.

I was in big trouble. Mack and I had been receiving payments that we were not entitled to. She told me they had received information that we were illegally claiming a sole-parent pension. She went on to tell me that I could possibly end up in jail, as the overpayment was a staggering $30,000. I realized this information would have come from our old landlord after we took off without paying the rent we owed.

After facing a panel for the overpayment, the decision was made to let me pay it back in instalments, rather than have me serve a jail sentence. This reduced my weekly payments to a pathetically small amount, yet at the time I considered myself lucky because I was profiting $1,000 a day dealing heroin.

Dealing heroin was risky business, and as a dealer, I had to be strategic. Having lived on the streets, I was streetwise and aware of the cops and their tactics. We had two golden rules in place.

First, there was to be no traffic at our house. This meant that we were never to deal drugs from home and no one was to approach our home for drugs.

Second, we would never carry the dealing phone while out dropping off drugs. Instead we had a spare phone, which we used to communicate between ourselves. The work phone stayed at home. This way, if we were caught with the drugs, there was no phone or evidence to say we were dealing.

We also knew there were people out there who wanted to ram-raid and rob us, so we equipped ourselves with a .22 calibre rifle, which we kept fully loaded, hidden behind the kitchen door.

Because of our lifestyle, I now kept away from my family, but they would often call around.

One day my dad came for a visit, concerned about my health. "Are you all right? Are you dying?"

My father had tears in his eyes. I was frightened and wondered if I really looked that bad. Yet despite what my dad was asking, I continued to sell and use drugs.

By now my tolerance was horrendously high. We were using a gram of heroin in one hit, which was costing $3,000 a day, and at that amount, we did not need the methadone anymore.

Early one morning, I was out dropping off deals when I decided to pull up at a local deli for some milk before heading back home. I was driving slowly into a parking bay when suddenly, out of nowhere, a man reached into my driver's side window, grabbing hold of the steering wheel while the car was still rolling to park.

"Turn it off! Turn it off!" he yelled at me.

"Okay, okay," I said, turning off the ignition.

I was freaking out because I thought I was being robbed. Then I looked the angry man in the face and realized it was the same detective who had raided me twice before.

(He and another detective had been keeping the deli under surveillance. I had no idea it was a hot spot for cops. This particular detective seemed to have it in for me, probably because I got off a jail term when I claimed I had given up drugs; he had not believed my claim and was very determined to bust me again.)

Damn it! I thought. *I'm still on the ISO for another couple of months.*

"Slowly get out of the car with your hands on your head," he demanded.

My eyes welled up with tears as he commenced to search my car. Without searching too hard, he found two packets of heroin tucked under my car seat cover.

"Thought you gave it up? Hah!"

He dangled the two packets in my face, making fun of me. I began quietly sniffling and crying as he read out my rights. As he continued, another detective cuffed my hands behind my back.

"Where's Mack?" he asked.

I was trying to come up with another story to get out of it lightly, so I told him Mack didn't know I was using again. All of a sudden my phone started ringing, and the detective looked curiously at me.

"It's only Mack wondering where I am," I said.

No one else knew my number. It was the private number we used to stay in touch. The detective thought he had me for dealing and reached into my back pocket to answer the phone.

"Hello, Mack! We have your lady here. We've just caught her with heroin again, but you wouldn't know anything about that now, would you?"

They took me down to the station and charged me with possession. I was in breach of my ISO, which meant I would face court for all those charges again, but surprisingly, after several hours they let me go.

"Where's my phone?" I asked the detective.

"I'm keeping it overnight, just to make sure you're not lying again," he said.

When I finally got back home that afternoon, Mack told me he had been getting calls all day from people chasing gear, and I needed to score again. Two more eight-balls of heroin were dropped off, tightly wrapped for easy disposal, and I sold one ball that night. The next morning, I was woken by the sound of knocking at my back door.

When I opened the door, I found myself face to face with the detective again. He was returning my phone. Suddenly I realized I was still holding the second eight-ball of heroin in my hand.

"Hey, Angel, just returning your phone," he said.

He glanced around the house as I stood there calm and collected. I figured that after having my phone all day and night, he was convinced I was not selling drugs.

He handed me the phone and said, "Behave." Then he walked off back down my driveway. Once again, I was safe.

Deep down I knew the drugs were a curse. Life as a junkie was taking its toll. Mack appeared happy with our lifestyle but I was constantly getting the horrors and desperately looking for light at the end of my dark tunnel. I was so down about my lifestyle that one day I found myself complaining, expressing my thoughts to one of my female customers as I was giving her a lift home.

I raved on about how our country was swamped with the drug, expressing the hope that it would run out. I felt if that happened, we would all have some hope by being forced to give it up.

My complaint seemed more like a cry for help. It was as if I was talking to God. My passenger was hanging onto every word I said. Today she is my witness to what happened the next day.

The next morning, from five o'clock on, I received several phone calls from customers desperate to score. It was so bad that I had to turn my phone off while I went to score.

I got to our dealer's house, thinking I would pick up an ounce and intending to order another, but from my dealer's lips came the bad news that he had none! He did not know *when* he would have some again.

This was not good. Normally he was never out of supply for long. His news meant I needed to look elsewhere.

I went through my phone book looking for other dealers. Everyone I rang said no, and I could not seem to score anywhere. I went to fetch what was left of my personal bag, which weighed just over six and half grams. With our tolerances, that was not much.

In desperation I turned to God, remembering what I had said the day before while I was driving my girlfriend home. I thought, *This can't be happening.* What were the chances of my words becoming a reality? Was it a coincidence, or had God really heard my cry for help? Whatever it was it was happening, and it spelt disaster for us as a family and the entire heroin trade. (Anyone who has been an addict would know what kind of disaster I am talking about.) I looked up toward heaven and begged God to take back what I had said!

The shockwaves of a major hold-up in heroin supply were being felt across the continent. One organization, WASUA, produced a great article in their monthly magazine *YOOZ*, and they have given me permission to include excerpts here.

The Great Heroin Drought of 2001

Those of you who are heroin users may have found it very difficult to acquire your heroin lately. I know I have! There are a number of theories getting around the place at the moment, but far be it for me to give you the exact reason for the lack of supply. I thought I could talk about some of these theories here.

The one I have heard the most is that because this Chinese year is the year of the snake, supposedly no business can be done between the end of Jan. and the end of Feb. I can still buy bread and milk etc. from all the local Asian delis, so I am a bit dubious about this story ...

Secondly, six months ago, Kun Sa, the most powerful warlord in Burma, who controls the opium trade in that region, has retired. Apparently we had enough stocks to last those six months, and now they are drying up.

Another one is that Afghanistan was offered a lot of money by the IMF (the International Monetary Fund) to reduce their opium crops. Again, doubtful, but hey—stranger things have happened.

The Chinese government has just admitted that there has been a recent explosion in heroin users, (600,000 to 800,000), so much of the supply is being diverted up there. Lastly, and this seems like this most probable, is that there was a huge, and we are talking huge, bust in Fiji a few months ago. This apparently was bound for Australia.

So there you have it. The theories around the great heroin drought ... So all we can do is lay in wait and hope the drought ends soon.

Rain-dances, or in this case dope-dances, could not hurt, I suppose!

*****LATE NEWS!!!!!!!!!!!!!!!!

It has been reported that someone brought some heroin. It was shit and very expensive, but, hey! It's a start! …

(The purpose of WASUA is to support the "yoozer." Their website and magazine contain all the latest gossip, advice on how to use drugs safely, and gives information on programs, treatments for hepatitis C sufferers, street-based sex workers, and mums on drugs. Mack and I would go to their centre every week to exchange six hundred dirty needles for six hundred clean ones. The people who worked there were very caring and supportive.)

During the heroin drought, the lack of heroin brought desperate people from all over to our front door, people we had never seen or dealt to before—even some Vietnamese who could barely speak English. We later learned they were connected to the Triad mafia.

Anyone and everyone who had anything to do with heroin was affected. People came together to talk about the problem and what had caused it.

We finally learned that two large shipping containers of drugs coming into Australia had been busted. This was enough to cause the massive drought. There would still have been heroin around, but people were sitting on it because any traffic would attract the cops.

Scores of people rallied at our place, where we all anxiously waited for a phone call that would tell us where we might be able to score. By morning, our lounge floor was covered with people who had crashed out, waiting. Those who could not wait lay with their bodies curled up tight in the foetal position, riddled with the agonizing symptoms of withdrawal. Thankfully, by eleven o'clock there was hope and the phone rang with news that there were going to be packets for sale, in an hour's time, at a nearby park.

The meeting place was like a mad-sale rush, with hundreds of people hanging to score. The packets on offer were mostly sugar and it was costing a fortune. In just one day, we spent close to $3,000 on packets trying to get stoned. It was no use, and we were running out of money fast. I decided to buy an ounce of speed to keep the money turning over, but I was spending it faster than I could make it. There was no relief from the anguish. The drought forced many people to give up the fight and book themselves into rehab centres while others went doctor shopping for prescription substitutes.

At this point, my speed dealer offered to get us a *grey nurse*, the street name for a one hundred milligram morphine tablet. I asked him what they were like.

"Hell yeah," he said. "You'll get smashed off them, even better than grade-A smack!"

I was pretty excited when I heard that! A strip of ten pills was worth $250, but if you sold them separately, they were $50 each. The pills needed to be heated in a tablespoon of water and crushed, after which a huge filter had to be used because they contained a lot of wax, which you did *not* want in your blood stream!

After my first shot of the morph, I experienced a very weird and intense feeling of pins and needles through my entire body, followed by a much-welcomed relief from the pain of withdrawal, and then finally a peaceful, stoned, intoxicated feeling where I was in "heaven" and comfortably numb.

We must have gone into a deep sleep on the lounge because the next thing I remember was waking up to a series of loud bangs on our front door, which was opposite from where we were sitting. I did not register the first bang straight away, but by the second bang, I was opening my eyes and trying to focus. By the third bang, I saw the white powder and bits of plaster falling from the top edge of the doorframe. I did not know what to think. I was still trying to comprehend the situation.

At the fourth bang, the door burst open and in charged some men dressed in black, wearing balaclavas and carrying high-powered guns.

"Freeze!" they screamed.

CHAPTER TEN

Nowhere to Run

"Move ... move ... move!"

The men dressed in black were a tactical response group.

Mack and I were hauled off the lounge chair and rushed out to the kitchen, where they forced us to the floor face-down, handcuffing us while the rest searched the remainder of the house. I could not believe what was happening. It was all happening so fast.

I was lying flat on the floor with my face turned to my right when I saw a syringe under one of the kitchen chairs. The needle was sticking up out of the linoleum. It was full of morph and blood, blocked by the cooling wax. I heard one of them pull open the door of the cupboard, where we kept the loaded rifle. Under the sink in the kitchen cupboard they found the box containing six hundred used, bloody syringes.

"We have no drugs, there's a drought!" I kept telling them, but they were not listening. They continued to search our house for drugs that we did not have.

Two undercover female cops arrived to assist the children to school. I felt sickened as I thought about the environment I had created for my three children. It was abuse—outright child abuse!

The cops were laughing and making jokes about what they were finding in our bedroom drawers. They made a mess of our house, and I prayed they would not find the bag containing gold and a very expensive diamond hidden under the dirty laundry in the washing machine.

By lunchtime I was starting to feel sick, needing my hit. I knew I was not going to get it because I was going for a ride back to the station to be charged, processed, and locked up. I was in for a painful few days and was really spinning out. "God, help me!" I prayed.

I asked one of the detectives if I could light up a fag and he made us go and sit in the bedroom while they kept on searching. As we walked into the bedroom, I spotted a little red tablet sitting next to the foot of our ensemble bed. My eyes lit up, and I had to dive for it and devour it before the cops could stop me.

(This tablet was a drug used for alcohol withdrawal, but it takes the edge off heroin withdrawal as well. Imagine how I felt when I saw that little red pill. It was a case of "Yes! Thank you, Lord!" Without it, I would have been in for a very bad night.)

The men kept searching, as they were sure we had something. Four hours later the detectives were still digging up my backyard. Finally one of them said, "There's nothing here; let's call it a day."

By this time, my yard was a mess. They escorted us out to the police car, carrying with them the loaded rifle and the used syringes.

One of the detectives turned to me. "Next time we raid you, we'll have to use tear-gas, all because of this loaded gun."

Off we went to the station.

Surprisingly, they released us both on personal bail with a set date to appear in court. That's when I realized we had been charged with possession of *two* dangerous weapons, not one. The syringe full of blood was considered a weapon, as the blood could have been contaminated with a disease, which it was!

The next day we received an eviction notice in our mail, giving us two weeks to vacate the premises. Suddenly it was déjà vu as I realized I was in the same mess as I had been two years ago. I was miserable, and the only thing that made it go away was to get stoned and forget about it, for a little while anyway, at least until the drug wore off.

That afternoon after returning from the police station, my new speed dealer, Snake, was waiting for us. He said he had a surprise for me. I was hoping it was a nice taste of heroin, but instead he pulled out a bag of what he called crack cocaine, along with a glass pipe. I had never seen anything like this before. He dropped a crystal rock into the glass pipe.

"Here, try this; you'll love it. This will take all your cares away," he said, passing me the pipe and lighter.

I put the pipe to my mouth and ignited the lighter. I carefully placed the flame beneath the bowl of the pipe and watched as the crystal began to melt into a liquid and the bowl filled with smoke. I inhaled the smoke, holding it in while I watched the liquid slowly return to crystal form as it cooled down. Then an intense stone came over me, much like the stone you get from smack except with a dizzy, weird feeling. I did not really like it that much, but it was a drug and for a little while it stopped me thinking about the fact that my $20,000 was all gone and so was my daily supply of heroin.

For two years, I had managed to turn it over daily, but all that I had left now was a bag of gold and a diamond that was red hot. There was nobody with that kind of money or drugs to trade for them. We were doomed. Every day we would go out to the pawnbrokers and hock enough for a day's supply.

It was hard being an addict. Trying to find the money to support addiction is a task in itself, especially when you are as sick as a dog and hanging for a shot. We lived and breathed heroin. We were nothing without it. The only thing that mattered when I woke up in the morning was my shot and where it was coming from. If there was no shot, we were bedridden in a sea of wet sheets and acute anxiety.

We took each day as it came, and every day was a challenge that seemed harder than the one before.

One afternoon we returned from selling some gold and were both exhausted, not to mention hanging for a fix. We dropped our backpacks by the door and sat at the kitchen table to mix a shot. At some point we both nodded off. My head was resting on the kitchen table.

Suddenly I was woken by the sound of a loud thud at the back door and was stunned to see three big Indigenous fellas come barging in.

"Give us your money and your drugs!" they yelled at us.

My immediate response was to grab the half pool cue leaning against the wall and charge at them with it. When I did, they took off out back, grabbing my bags off the floor as they went. Puzzled at their reaction, I scratched my head and then realized with horror that they had bolted off with the bag, the one containing the gold and the diamond worth $10,000.

I thought, *Now what?* With the gold and the diamond gone, we were stuck with a raging morphine habit and no way to support it.

Days later the real-estate agent visited us. Our time to vacate had expired and they served us with a court action to evict us. We could not rent anywhere as we were blacklisted and were due to appear in court the following day.

When morning arrived, we purposely didn't go to court, as we were afraid of being locked up. A bench warrant was issued for our arrest.

As if that was not enough, the real-estate agent came and changed all the locks on the house, locking all our stuff inside. We were now homeless.

Every day was a struggle to find somewhere to sleep. Each day, if we made a profit from dealing, we could pay for a motel. If not, we had no choice but to break into the house we'd vacated and squat (illegal occupancy) for the night. Our belongings were there, packed in boxes, but we had nowhere to go. Considering the mess our lives were in, it was a miracle that our children were still with us and had not been taken away by Welfare.

The following day we dropped the kids off at school and headed back over to the house in an attempt to move our things out. We loaded our station wagon to the roof racks, but as we were reversing, we noticed a paddy wagon at the front and the cops knocking at the door.

Mack and I panicked, as we knew what this meant. When they saw us reversing, they came running down the steps toward us, signalling with their hands to stop. We had no choice but to stop and face our fate.

A police officer asked me my name to confirm who I was. Then he leaned in to look at who was driving. "Mack?"

"Yep." He nodded.

"Turn the car off, mate. Just step out of the vehicle real slow and put your hands on your head. Thanks," one of the officers said. "You know what we are here for?"

They made us lock the car and escorted us to the back of the paddy wagon, where they told us, "You guys have a bench warrant for your arrest, and we're taking you both to court to face the magistrate."

Hours later, I was down in the holding cells of the courthouse. The walls surrounding me were covered in graffiti. I sat there on the hard wooden bench, anxiously waiting. School was out in less than an hour, and I needed to be there to pick up my kids.

Finally, somebody was coming for me. The footsteps headed straight for my cell, and then I heard the sound of the key turning in the lock. I knew that sound all too well.

"Your turn," the female officer said. She escorted me down the hall and into the courtroom, where I took a seat beside Mack.

As the charges were read out, I stood with my hands behind my back and a long face.

When the magistrate learned that we had failed to appear in court a week ago, he spoke very sternly to us. "You will both be remanded in strict custody for two weeks."

My jaw dropped. I was going to jail for fourteen days?

I started panicking, as the time was two thirty. As I left the courtroom, I begged the officer to let me make a phone call. I explained my circumstances, and she gave me permission to ring my mum and sister, but when I rang, there was no answer. I was then taken back to my cell, where I cried out to God, asking that

He protect, comfort, and somehow lead my kids to safety, as they would be wondering where we were.

Finally, at six forty-five that evening, I arrived at the women's prison. I was feeling sick with worry. I asked the officers processing me if they had heard anything about my children, but they had heard nothing.

I turned to God in prayer, begging him to take care of my children. An inner voice assured me, saying, *Don't worry; all will be okay.*

God's voice had a calming effect on the storm raging within me. While I sat quietly in that peace, the phone rang with information that my children were with my mother and that I would be able to call as soon as the processing was complete. My faith in God soared to a completely new level.

Strangely, I was grateful to be in jail. I viewed it as a blessing in disguise. I could rest and get well again. My body was suffering terribly due to my lifestyle. Stepping on the scales, I weighed in at only forty-five kilograms. I was skin and bones and severely withdrawing from heroin. The prison doctor saw me and put me on two lots of strong medication for five days, to help with the withdrawals. I was so lethargic I could not stand. I only felt good when I was lying down, getting up only for muster and meal times. As I lay there, I would think of how much I missed my kids and Mack. (Mack was in a men's jail somewhere else.)

Jail was never the place I had wanted to end up. I had managed to stay out of it up to that point. Spider's family had threatened me that if I ever set foot in the jail, I would cop it! Now here I was. Numerous members of his family occupied cells in the west end of the quadrangle, and some of them were in cells right next to the office where everyone went to pick up their mail each day.

One morning I went to collect my mail. I was still so weak I could barely stand. Without any warning I was punched from behind and sent flying into the hard brick wall. The guards rushed to my aid when they saw blood gushing from my eye and took me off to the nurses' station for stitches. It had happened so fast. I did not have to ask *why* it had happened. That was old news. This time I was too weak physically to fight back.

Four days later, I was sitting in the quadrangle, absorbing the morning sun and reading a letter from Mack. It was sweet, telling me how much he loved and missed me. I received permission to make my first phone call to my mum, but when I called her, all she did was rouse on me, as mothers do.

On day six, I was moved into a four-bed cell that I would share with three other girls. It was good to have some company. I was starting to feel a little better and didn't mind being locked up. I was especially pleased, knowing my kids were in safe hands.

I had been in jail for eleven days and was feeling heaps better, starting to get my strength back. The chick who had hit me apologized, and I let it slide. I do not hold grudges, and I only had three days to go before I went back to court.

Very soon it was day fourteen, and I was in a prison van on my way to the courthouse, very excited about getting out of jail.

After waiting down in the cells for hours, I finally saw Mack. We stood together before the magistrate, who appeared to be in a good mood. We hoped he was in a good enough mood to grant us bail, but when we looked around, there was no one to give us support or bail us out, which meant we were both going back to jail.

As soon as I got back to the jail, I was straight on the phone, asking my mum if she would provide bail, even though I knew she would refuse, which she did. I wondered who I could possibly ring. I did not have my phone book, and the only number that came to mind was my speed dealer, Snake.

I was not keen on the idea of ringing Snake. His glass eye and heavily scarred body gave me the creeps. Nevertheless he was my only hope, but when I phoned he also said no.

Surprised by his answer, I began begging, promising to cook and clean for him. Eventually he gave in and said he would be there to pick me up later that night.

Afterward, I lay in my cell. Strangely, a big part of me did not want to go. However, I had to, because Mack was relying on me to get him out.

By eleven that night Snake was there, just as he'd said. The first thing he did once we got back to his place was offer me a taste of speed. He loved his speed but was totally against the heroin.

After our hit, we talked for most of the night. By three he started to get a little weird on me, telling me to have a bubble bath. When I said no, he got upset and offered me another taste of whizz. Maybe he thought he could drug me into doing what he wanted, but I was determined to stay one step ahead of him. I pretended to have the whizz, squirting it past my arm and into the sink behind me.

Snake watched me like a hawk.

By this time I was starting to feel extremely uncomfortable.

His phone was ringing hot with customers, but for some reason he wasn't answering it. Then I heard a familiar voice coming from the TV, and I went to suss it out. It was a famous preacher, and he was preaching about fear. I was intrigued and sat down to listen.

Next thing, Snake walked in from the kitchen. He was holding a handgun and began showing it off, pointing out the beaming red laser attached to it.

"See that red dot on the wall? That's where the bullet goes."

Talk about fear! I was feeling it all right!

By now I was truly frightened and did not know which way to look. I glanced at the wall. The red dot was not there. Shivers ran up and down my spine, but I plucked up courage and just looked straight at him as he juggled the gun nervously from one hand to the other. Shortly after, he went hurrying back to the kitchen.

I cannot express in words what I was feeling. All I know is that my mind was racing. What had just happened terrified me.

I was seriously wondering if he was intending to shoot me. I was freaking out, and the drugs were making the paranoia worse. I felt surrounded by a very eerie feeling. On top of that, a terrible smell was wafting in from the backdoor.

As I sat wondering what the awful smell was, Snake's dog came charging in with a huge rotten bone and tried to hide it behind the lounge.

"Here, boy," I heard Snake call from the kitchen. He whistled and the dog went to him.

It sounded like Snake was playing with his dog in the kitchen, so I got up, thinking it would be a good time to join them. I hoped that by doing so, it would change the thick, eerie atmosphere that had followed the gun episode.

As I walked into the kitchen, I saw Snake on his hands and knees, eating out of the dog's bowl. Shocked, I backed out quickly and quietly, holding my breath over what I had just witnessed. I crept slowly back to my chair.

Snake began talking to himself, and I heard him slamming cupboard doors. I sensed he was angry, and when he insisted aloud that I take a bath and go to sleep, I had a feeling that that was not all he was wanting.

I lay on the lounge, pretending to be asleep. I had never seen this side of him before and I was scared. He was acting like a psychopath, capable of anything. Feeling I was in danger, I started praying to God. Before I could say amen, I heard Snake leave the kitchen and go to his bedroom.

I waited anxiously for him to fall sleep, but instead I heard what sounded like Snake engaging in animal sex with his dog. I covered my head with pillows and blankets, trying to block out the gross sounds, wishing it was all a bad dream.

It felt like only minutes had passed while I was under those blankets, but in reality, I had laid there for two hours. Slowly I pulled off the covers and heard the sound of snoring coming from Snake's bedroom. He had finally fallen asleep.

I was busting to go to the toilet, and when I was done, I tiptoed around the house. It was now daylight. I wanted to see where the bad smell was coming from and went outside.

I was shocked to see heaps of dog poo piled up like furniture all the way to the backyard that was partly fenced off. I proceeded to look over and beyond the fence. What I saw was a huge mountain of rotting garbage, which looked and stank like the local tip. I thought it all very bizarre.

At this time, the news was reporting that a suspected serial killer was loose in the city. Three women (and possibly another) had disappeared in similar circumstances after attending night spots (clubs) in the area. Because the circumstances of each disappearance were much the same, police suspected that they were dealing with a serial killer. The last victim had been taken only weeks before my time in jail. Only two of the missing women's bodies had been found, in bushland on the outskirts of the city. With no leads on the killer, everyone was a suspect.

I recalled seeing numerous news flashes on a certain television program. In the program, the public was encouraged to come forward with any information, letting police know of anything or anyone that aroused suspicion. One of the things given out was that the killer would most likely have sheds in the backyard. Here in my dealer's backyard was a huge Demountable (transportable shed/ building).

I was not prepared to check it out, afraid of what might happen if he woke up and found me snooping.

Weird thoughts circulated in my mind, such as how the dumpster would be a great place to hide a body. The horrific smell in the air was definitely like something dead.

I walked slowly around the outside of the house and came across some rolls of carpet lying on the grass beside his little white ute. I thought it was odd that perfectly good rolls of carpet were outside in the weather like that. It then occurred to me that it was a perfect setup for transporting bodies. I remembered a report that mentioned a ute of that description having been seen in the bushland area around the time the second victim went missing.

I now felt strongly that there was something very fishy about Snake. I wondered if he was planning to kill me as well. After all, no one knew I was at his place, and he had not answered any of his calls all night.

Thoughts raced through my head. If he did kill me, no one would know about it. He could easily tell the cops I had run away, because that is exactly how I was viewed by the cops—a "runaway street kid."

With this thought in mind, I raced back inside to put on my shoes and take off before he woke up. As I was tying my shoelace, he stopped snoring and began coughing and spluttering. It was then that I heard that familiar inner voice say, *Relax; don't go. Offer him a coffee and stay.*

My incredulous response was, *What, God? You want me to do what?*

By this time, Snake was moving around. I heard the TV come on, so I asked if he wanted a cuppa. He was watching some morning show that was talking about Mother's Day. Mother's Day? Crap! If it was Mother's Day, I wanted to go and see my mum!

I walked into his room carrying a hot coffee and sat on a chair beside his bed. A breaking news announcement about the serial killer had just interrupted the morning show. By now my fear had turned to anger. I became more daring.

"Who do you reckon is doing this and getting away with it?"

I asked this boldly, looking him square in the eyes.

"Not sure," he replied, dropping his head and disengaging from all eye contact.

I had been looking for this exact reaction. I recalled a time when he had told me about friends he had on the police force and how he would go to their police balls.

I asked myself, *Could he be in a position where no one would suspect him?* I was also thinking, *Is he friends with crooked cops?* I was very suspicious.

I felt evil vibes coming off the man. I wondered about the scars on his arms. Could he have gotten them from victims clawing him? What about his glass eye? Could one of the victims have clawed it out while trying to save herself? Could his reason for not wanting to stand bail be that he was afraid I might find him out, discover his secret?

I kept mulling things over, thinking back to when we had first met. I was looking for clues and answers to all the questions burning in my head. By now I was convinced Snake was guilty but decided to keep my cool about it until my court date, which was less than two weeks away. After drinking my last mouthful of coffee, I asked if he wouldn't mind if I went to visit my mother for Mother's Day.

"Yeah, no worries, I'll give you a lift," he replied.

On the way to Mum's, we stopped at a servo to buy flowers. When I got to her place, I smiled and waved him good-bye as if everything was normal.

As I made my way to the front door of my parent's house, I saw three little heads peeping from under the curtain on the window. It was my kids, and when they saw me, they yelled throughout the house.

"It's Mum! Mummy's back!"

As I approached the front door, I could smell the aroma of freshly percolated coffee lingering in the air.

"Knock-knock, it's Mum!" I sang out.

My three kids rushed to bear-hug me. They were so happy to see me.

"Happy Mother's Day, Mum!"

I handed my mum a great big bunch of freshly picked yellow flowers and hugged her, thanking her for all she was doing. Unlike my kids, Mum was not very happy to see me.

I could not really blame her. My parenting skills totally sucked. She looked at me with that same look she had always given me. It was that all-too-familiar "you're good for nothing" look, and in the heat of that moment, I lost it completely. Something in me just snapped.

I began shouting and crying, "I hope you're happy, Mum, because now a murderer knows where you live."

Out of nowhere, my youngest sister, Gianna, rushed me and tackled me to the ground. We fought until Mum broke us up with the broomstick. Mum had heard what I had yelled at her.

"What do you mean, a murderer?" she demanded.

I was in a stressed emotional state over all that had happened at Snake's, and I lashed out at Mum, blaming her for the situation I was now in with Snake.

"That man who just dropped me off could well be that serial killer, and now he knows where you live. It's all because *you* refused to help me! Maybe if you cared enough, I might wake up to myself. Look who's pulled me out of the shit this time!"

Mum and Gianna looked at me in disbelief. I stormed out the door, leaving my kids behind, knowing Mum would take care of them. I was angry and hurt that my parents never seemed to care enough to help me. Tears streaming down my face, I walked until I hit the main highway and hitched a ride to my old house.

Everything had been left behind the day I was taken into custody. When I got there, I nearly died. My car was gone, along with everything I had packed in it. I tried to get into the house but was unable to, as the locks had been changed. I went round to the window and found it smashed. I looked in and saw everything we owned trashed and scattered on the floor. I climbed through the window, careful not to cut myself, and once inside I saw that a box containing my children's baby photos and portraits was missing. The only things remaining were the furniture items I had bought with my compensation payout two years ago. I was so angry by it all and desperately needed Mack.

I needed to get him out of jail somehow, but it meant going back to the heroin, and there was only one person in that scene who could help me, if I begged enough. After all, bailing out a junkie is taking a huge risk, and in this case a $3,000 risk if Mack jumped court. I headed toward the north side of the city to visit an old mate, a Vietnamese Triad leader who, since the drought, sold the best smack in town. After meeting up with him and explaining my situation, he agreed to help, but he also warned me of the consequences if Mack jumped bail.

While he went off to bail Mack out, I went back to the house to try to sort our things out. I had butterflies as I waited for Mack to arrive, and when he finally did, I ran outside to meet him. We hugged and kissed, showing just how much we had missed each other. Mack looked around the yard and asked where our car was.

"I don't know. It was gone when I got here. It's obvious someone pinched it, but wait till you see what someone's done inside."

I watched as Mack walked in the house to find half our things missing and the rest scattered everywhere. Without speaking, we rallied together to clean and salvage what was left, both of us feeling despair clouding over us. In reality, we were in a hopeless situation. We had no car and nowhere to stay and were desperate to get our stuff out of this house. As it was, we were risking our freedom by being there. The cops had made it clear that we would be trespassing if we went there. After cleaning up the mess, we locked the house as best we could and went to Mum's to pick up the kids.

That afternoon we found ourselves wandering aimlessly around shopping centres until closing time. We raided charity bins for warm clothing before breaking into an empty government housing home for a place to sleep. We huddled together on the floor for body warmth and used the clothes we had stolen from the clothing bins as blankets.

As I lay in that empty house, I could not help but feel bad about the situation we were in. I whispered to my children how sorry I was and how, in the morning I would take them to a place where they would be looked after, with food, shelter, and a warm bed—just until we found a place of our own.

In the darkness, my oldest son Baron refused the offer. "No, Mum, we don't care; we want to stay with you." My heart just sank.

"Good night, sweetheart," I whispered.

In the morning I woke as Mack returned from a trip to the shops. It was both our paydays, and he had brought back chocolate milk for breakfast, the local paper, and a packet of smokes. After looking in the for-sale section, he found a van selling for $800, exactly the amount we had between us. We all ran to the shops for a cab so we could go look at it. When we got there, the car salesman was very kind, telling us the van owner only owed him $400, and he was happy to let it go for that price. Shouting at the top of my lungs, I praised God! Now we had shelter and $400 left to live on.

That reddish-brown van became our home. The backseats folded down into beds for the kids, and we were able to keep warm as we drove around with the heater on before pulling up at a nearby park and calling it a night. We were woken up many times by cops shining their torches through the fogged-up windows. Once they realized we were a homeless family, they left us alone and moved on.

The next morning, in the hope of getting a house, I applied for emergency housing. We harassed them daily and even slept right outside the office to make a point of our desperate situation.

Four months passed, and we were still living in our van. Just when I thought I could not go on for another day like this, we got the call to come and pick up the keys to our very own three-bedroom townhouse. This was the greatest news ever, and it could not have come at a better time, as I was due to appear in court the following Monday. I had needed an address.

Finally, the day of the court appearance was upon me. I was given a twelve-month suspended sentence for possession of heroin. Once again I just scraped through, as I had breached my ISO order. It was obvious to me God was choosing to show His favour and grace.

Now that court was over, I was no longer tied to Snake through bail, but I would still have a lot to do with him, as he was my main speed dealer. Through this connection, I was also able to monitor him. I still suspected he might be the serial killer.

CHAPTER ELEVEN

The Missing Piece

Days later I was off to score some speed from Snake. When I got to his place, he was not there but a bunch of youths was raiding his home. He always had young street kids hanging around, but today seemed a little out of the ordinary.

Not wanting to have anything to do with what I had seen, I quickly left the house and got back in my car. I reversed out of the driveway, but just as I was about to drive off, one of the boys, who I knew, came running out to my car yelling, "Stop!" He opened the back door and jumped in, puffing, panting, and nervously nursing a bag in his arms.

As I drove off, he started to pull things out of it. He claimed the bag had been hidden in Snake's shed.

"What's this?" he asked. He had pulled out what looked like a police uniform.

I pulled over to the side of the road, very curious to find out who the uniform belonged to. As he unfolded it, a cop's badge fell out onto the floor, as well as a passport wallet containing a card that had a picture of Snake posing as an acting officer. The young fella and I looked at each other, puzzled.

"He's a nark," the young fella said.

By now I was really tripping and lost for words. My head was racing with all kinds of theories and questions.

Could this be another missing piece of the puzzle?

Why did he have a cop's uniform if he was not a cop?

If he was not a cop, how did he acquire it?

Had he used the uniform to gain easier access to the women?

I thought hard about this find and realized the discovery of the uniform was the icing on the cake for me. I knew I could not keep it to myself any longer.

I stood in a shopping centre, staring at the phone booths, very scared to make the call, scared to pass on all the information I had been carrying around.

Why? Firstly, I was staunch, never giving information to cops, and secondly, I was scared that Snake might find out it was me. However, as I stood there hesitating, I heard that quiet voice inside say, *If you don't make the call, you will be held accountable for the lives of many other victims.*

I immediately knew what I needed to do and how important it was to report him. I psyched myself up and went ahead, making the call to the special number given on the television program.

I nervously waited, listening to the ringing tone. When the officer answered, I told her what I knew and suggested they go check it out. I stayed anonymous until she insisted I tell her how I knew all this. She asked me three times, each time interrupting me while I was speaking.

That was when I began to get angry. I could not understand what it was that she wanted to know. After all, according to the program, the police were asking for people with any relevant information to come forward and to me, my information was very relevant. The sheds and the Demountable in the backyard, plus the police uniform with Snake's name on it should have been enough information.

Instead I felt interrogated by this woman, and that was when I exploded, yelling at her, "I know all this because he bailed me out of jail and I've been staying in his home!"

As soon as the words were out of my mouth, I realized I had blown my cover. The woman did not say another word, but she gave me a reference number I could use to follow up the enquiry.

Every day I drove by Snake's home, anxious to see any signs of police activity. One morning I noticed the white ute had disappeared from the front yard. I quickly drove home to call the number again so I could find out what was going on. They told me that forensics had taken the ute for investigation.

Now all I could do was wait and listen for any information to come from the radio or TV news.

For weeks I waited and waited, but there was none. I was making myself sick worrying about it and later found out that the sickness was also partly because I was twelve-weeks pregnant.

As if that news was not bad enough, Mack was apprehended and taken back to jail for outstanding warrants. I was now alone with my three kids and devastated about being on drugs while I was pregnant. This spelt disaster for my unborn child and me.

With Mack gone, I was worried how I was going to get my next shot, but I managed to survive after meeting a guy old enough to be my father who had a huge supply of morph. I was buying two or three sheets of morph a day and selling them like hotcakes. I had plenty of money to get by and lots of personal (drugs).

This was always the way when Mack was not around. The minute Mack was out again, we were back to scraping for all our needs. I guess you could say I was wise when it came to wheeling and dealing. Maybe it rubbed off from my parents, who were very good at saving.

Two months later and it was my thirtieth birthday, and Mack was still locked up in remand. I was alone and slumped over my kitchen table after a big birthday shot. I worried about my kids. I knew I was unable to parent them in the state I was in. God knew where they were—probably running the streets somewhere.

Some nights my two boys, Baron, age twelve, and Steele, age ten, did not come home. My girl, Carina, at the tender age of eight, often stayed with a friend she had made in the area.

I slowly pulled myself up out of the slump and sat up, feeling very stoned and down on myself. My baby moved inside me, which depressed me even more, but then I felt a supernatural presence surrounding me. I had felt the same presence in my youth. I knew it well. I would always sense it whenever I was alone and sad, and in that moment, I cried out to God.

"Lord, help me. I'm on heroin and now I'm pregnant. What am I going to do?"

I knew being on heroin could kill my baby, and I begged God to forgive me. For a moment, there was nothing more than a hopeless silence, and then a voice said to me, *It's okay. Everything is going to be fine. You'll see.*

The voice of God always brought comfort to me, and after hearing those words, I clung to His assurance. There was nothing else positive that I could cling to. I was living in fear of my and my child's future, and God's voice was a mountain of hope to me.

I somehow knew I was of worth to Him even though I felt worthless. I began to believe that things would really be okay, even though reality was shouting the opposite. Yes, God was the only one I could turn to.

I could not go to the doctor, out of fear I would be judged and possibly have all my children taken away. Worse still, the doctor would automatically put me back on methadone for the baby's sake, as heroin withdrawal can cause the death of the unborn child.

Methadone is a synthetic heroin regulated by the government, designed to stop junkies from hanging out (sick with withdrawal symptoms). Once on methadone, it is very hard to get off it. It was for this reason that I chose to trust God.

(There were days when I was hanging out for a fix and I felt my baby pushing outward under stress. It was obvious to me that my baby was also feeling the pain of withdrawal.)

Early one evening I was waiting for my kids to return home from their play when the phone rang. I thought it was a customer, but to my shock and surprise, it was Snake. I had not seen him since I had moved into my unit, and now he was asking where I was because he had something to discuss with me.

"What's your address?" he asked.

I panicked at the question. With Mack in jail and no one to protect me, I was too scared to tell him, knowing his reason for wanting to talk. I hesitated before giving him a false address.

He rang back thirty minutes later, frustrated because he could not find me. He asked again for my address, but I did not say anything.

"I heard you dobbed me in!"

The second he said that, I hung up!

Now I was petrified. If he was not the serial killer, why did he just say that? I thought hard about how he could have known. No one else but those working that special hotline knew. I had the strong feeling Snake was now going to come looking for me.

As days went by, I feared for my life. Every knock on the door had me panicking. I was living in a state of fear and paranoia. I wanted to leave but had nowhere to go. I started keeping people with me at all times.

At night I felt that there was someone outside my house. One night this feeling was so strong I dropped to the floor and crawled to the other side of the room. I reached up with one arm to turn off the lights. Once the lights were off, I had a good look outside before closing the curtains again and switching the lights back on.

Everyone around me thought I had gone completely mad. Call it what you like, but I was not taking any chances. Even having a shot was risky because being stoned would put me off-guard. However, with all that was happening, I desperately needed a shot to calm me down.

Standing in front of the bathroom mirror, I studied myself intensely, looking at what I had become. Dark shadows circled my eyes; in my hand was a syringe full of hot, waxy, freshly mixed morphine. I raised it up before my face and turned my head to the left so I could see the vein more clearly. By this time, all the veins in my arms had collapsed, and the vein in my neck was my only hope. I gazed at myself in the mirror. I was deeply aware the morphine would go straight to my brain, and the thought that I might have missed some wax when I filtered filled me with concern.

"This could kill me, Lord," I whispered anxiously.

In that moment, I heard God's voice *thunder* these words: "You are *never* going to die!"

His words echoed and rolled, the way thunder echoes in a storm-filled sky. I didn't really understand the full meaning of what He was saying (I would learn this further down the track), but I believed in my God and I believed the words He had just spoken to me. I *knew* the shot I was about to have was *not* going to kill me.

The day finally came when Mack was due to appear in court. He would, more than likely, be released, after spending the last three months in custody.

That afternoon, after carefully answering a knock at our door, I was ecstatic to see Mack standing there. I jumped on him, happy to have him back with me. I told all the people who were hanging round in our house to leave—they were not needed anymore. Mack was home.

I told him everything that had happened with Snake, but he did not believe the part where I sensed that Snake was outside scoping me out from the back fence. He also thought a "gut feeling" was not enough evidence to believe Snake was out there.

Later that night we were in our room mixing up a shot and talking about it when suddenly I shushed Mack.

"There's someone outside," I whispered as I pointed at the window.

"Bull crap. You're just paranoid," Mack replied.

Suddenly there was a knock on my window. Mack jumped and nearly stabbed himself with his pick. I freaked out too because I had started believing that perhaps Mack was right—I was "only stressing out." Then we heard a voice.

"It's me, Luella. Could I borrow some sugar?"

I sighed with relief. It was only my neighbour.

However, it proved that my gut feelings were accurate. There really had been someone there. Thankfully it was only Luella, but what if it had been Snake with plans to shoot me!

Early the following morning I heard a noise outside my flat. I ran to check it out and found a man from the electricity company. He was in the process of switching off my power. I had not paid my $500 bill. The look on my face must have said it all. He just looked at me and said, "Sorry, I'm just doing my job."

No electricity meant no hot water and no way of heating anything up. It also left us having to use candles as a form of light at night.

Having Mack home again meant another habit to feed. The pills and profits we made from selling were running out fast. To make things worse, our phone got stolen yet again, which made dealing drugs very difficult. Each time we got a new phone it would take weeks for everyone to get to know our new number. No customers meant no drugs, as we would use from the profits we made.

Desperation caused us to take big risks, like making up dud grams of heroin out of pills that took away leg cramps.

Desperate times called for desperate measures.

The next day we had two very angry customers walk in our front door with crowbars and knives demanding money and drugs. After robbing us of our dole payments and a few pills, we were left with absolutely nothing. This meant we had to start stealing again to feed our habits.

We would drive to shopping centres, to shoplift items that we could take back for refunds. Day in and day out we would do this, all the while feeling ill and desperately hanging for a fix.

I remember days when I fought with Mack because I could not do it anymore. I was eight months' pregnant and had no energy.

Mack was forced to look at other places such as big hardware stores for items like quality brand-name tool kits. Our morph dealers paid well for them.

You may be asking yourself, why did I start using again after getting out of jail clean, and why didn't I stay clean?

The truth is the drugs were not the issue. If the drugs were taken away, the underlying problem remained—I was hurting on the inside and had been hurting deeply for many years. The drugs were simply a form of self-medication.

I would question myself on the how-to (of getting over these emotional hurts) and the where-to-begin (when it came to getting real help). The answers always seemed to be—no way and nowhere.

I felt hopeless and went through bouts of deep depression, feeling down and questioning God. "Why am I here in this situation when I don't want to be? Help me, Lord!"

This was my cry so many times, but nothing ever happened. There seemed to be no escape. My addictive lifestyle went on, getting to the point where my body could not take the abuse any longer.

My legs became extremely swollen from my thighs all the way down to my toes. My neighbour would cuss at me to go to hospital because according to her I had toxaemia from the pregnancy.

Deep down I knew the swelling had more to do with the massive heroin addiction, because out of the pores of my skin came a funny-looking clear fluid that would run down my legs.

With no due date that I could go by, I knew within myself that my baby was going to arrive any day now. Sure enough, early one morning I woke up from a heavy heroin-induced sleep with a massive contraction underway. It was six thirty when I shook Mack awake and said, "Bubs (baby) is coming! Quick, mix up a shot and I'll call a cab."

When I got to the hospital, I was buckling over with contractions every four minutes. The nurse asked what was wrong and I told her I was in labour. She rushed me to a room where a doctor asked what he could do for me. I told him I was in labour with four-minute contractions.

"What? How far along are you?" he asked, looking at my belly.

"I'm full term," I replied.

He did not believe me because I was so small and there was no medical history of my pregnancy.

That was when I yelled, between contractions, "I'm a heroin addict!"

As soon as I said that I was rushed to a room where doctors and nurses surrounded me, one on each arm and leg. They were trying desperately to find a vein. There was a great deal going on and the pain was intense. It did not feel like I was there for very long before I gave birth, with the help of forceps, to our baby girl, who they rushed to intensive care.

We named her Storm, and when she was born she weighed only four pounds. I had been eating only ice, so she was malnourished.

The nurses were appalled. If looks could have killed, I would have died instantly on that delivery table. Yet their reactions were exactly as I had expected. While those critical eyes were on me I let myself drift to that peaceful place where God had assured me all would be well. I believed Him, and I was going to take Him at His word. I lay there with the judgment of the midwives pressing down on me, and turned my thoughts to God, focusing on His awesomeness instead.

That evening we were relocated to the hospital for children, where I was told my baby would not be able to leave the hospital until she put on a considerable amount of weight. They also told me it was going to take some time.

For the first couple of days of her life, I was worried about how my baby girl would cope with the withdrawal symptoms. My tolerance to heroin was so high that they had to administer morph to her to help her. Later they changed to a milder drug.

Throughout this time, I kept praying for her. I was thrilled to learn she had coped very well with the switch from one drug to another. Weeks later they stopped all the drugs completely. I had been so afraid she might not handle it, but she did really well.

I believe God's grace and unconditional love took care of her just as He said He would. She suffered hardly any withdrawals. I felt for other babies whose mothers were addicts. They suffered bad withdrawals and were very unsettled.

God was there for both of us. Despite the horrendous circumstances, He was there.

Only weeks later, after baby Storm was weaned off everything, I was contacted by children's services. They told me I had to do something about my heroin addiction before I could even think about taking my baby from the hospital.

The following day I went to a doctor who immediately put me on a special program. The program used a drug that is a long-acting opiate, primarily used to treat narcotic (opioid) dependence. The drug is sold as a pill that is dissolved under the tongue and its purpose is to prevent withdrawal symptoms from occurring by stimulating the opiate receptors in the brain and removing the desire to take heroin. I did not want to be on this treatment, but I did it to get my baby home.

Finally, after nine weeks of being in hospital, they let little Storm come home with us. I was so excited. Sadly, I continued to use heroin.

Our home was still without electricity. We were constantly asking the neighbours if we could warm up baby's bottle in their microwave. For her three o'clock feed, Mack would desperately light a fire out of twigs and sticks found around the yard and the pages from a phone book. This would take forever while I did everything possible to stop my baby from crying the neighbourhood down.

Even her baths were few and far between because no electricity meant no hot water. I would call my mum to come and take baby Storm home with her so she could have a bath there.

Life was tough, and none of my children deserved the hell we were putting them through.

CHAPTER TWELVE

A Close Call

One night we only had one solitary candle left. We decided we would stay together in one room and just go to sleep, seeing as the rest of the house was in darkness.

We threw all our mattresses on the lounge room floor, and bubby slept cosy in the pram I had stolen from the maternity ward the day we left the hospital. The lone candle was burning away on the TV set as we all drifted off to sleep.

Suddenly I jerked awake. I heard the sound of crackling sparks, and to my horror, large flames were shooting out of the TV. The room was quickly filling with black smoke and soot.

Mack frantically rushed to open the lounge room door but remembered that the door handle was missing. It had been broken for months, and we had been using a butter knife to open it. The knife was somewhere on the floor. Desperately he began hunting, feeling around for it.

"Hurry!" I yelled in panic.

Mack managed to locate the knife. Just in time too, as we could hardly breathe by this point. One by one we crawled out of the house. I was last, grabbing baby Storm on my way. Mack threw a blanket over the burning TV and raced it out, hurling it onto the front lawn. I watched, stunned at what had just happened, and counted my blessings. I gazed at baby's pram—it was covered in black soot. I was deeply thankful for the pram's hood, which had protected her throughout.

In the morning all the neighbours came over to see what had happened. It was pretty obvious as we stood about outside the flat, covered in black soot and very thankful to be alive.

The next day government housing officers came knocking on our door after receiving a report about the fire. Appalled at the state of the unit, they handed us an eviction notice and sternly told us to move out.

Right after they left, the cops arrived looking for Mack. To discourage them from looking further, I told them he had gone interstate, and they left. Mack had breached his ISO order, and this meant jail. I knew it was only a matter of time before they would be back looking for him.

During this time, my eldest son, Baron, was getting up to mischief with some local Indigenous kids. One of my customers told me Baron had been seen smoking marijuana and experimenting with speed. As if that wasn't enough, he was stealing property out of people's backyards.

That same afternoon I was dragged awake from my drug-induced sleep by a house full of intimidating elders of the local Indigenous tribe. They were cursing at me, demanding a bike that Baron had supposedly stolen from them. That was it! I had had enough! I decided to send Baron back east to live with his dad.

Saying good-bye to Baron as he boarded the plane was the hardest thing I have ever had to do, but seeing we were living such messed up lives, I felt it was the right course of action. I had noticed that people from government children's services had been hovering about, clearly after him. I hugged and kissed my Baron and then passed him his bag. The look on his face revealed his deep concern that he might never see us again. I reassured him that we would all be together again, just as soon as I could find a way to get us all there.

Deep down we both knew it was going to take a financial miracle, as we would need funds for five plane tickets in total. Nevertheless I was determined to get there, and it became my prayer that God would make a way.

With Baron now gone, life returned to the way it always was. There was never a moment when I did not think of him or wonder how I was going to make that trip back east.

It was just another ordinary day. Mack was feeding baby Storm a warm bottle of milk; it was the perfect picture—Daddy and his girl. I left for ten minutes to see how my neighbour Deb was doing with the packets of speed I had given her to sell. As I was leaving her place to go back to my flat, I saw, from her balcony, several cop cars surrounding our block of units. I quickly ran back home to find baby Storm on her own with an empty bottle beside her and no Daddy. She was all smiles and kicking her little legs around. I realized Mack had made a run for it. I picked baby up and went back over to Deb's where I could get a better view of the cops looking for Mack.

Minutes later I saw Mack, his hands cuffed behind his back. He was being escorted to a paddy wagon. I instantly felt the loss of Mack and wondered, *What am I going to do now?* I could not stay in the unit because it was not fit for living, and I had been evicted. Moreover, I was not going outside at three in the morning to light a fire for baby's bottle while she screamed the neighbourhood down. That was when I decided to go for a walk to visit an old guy named Ivan. Ivan had previously helped us with our van when it broke down. Over time we had become good friends.

After telling him that Mack was in lock-up and we had no electricity in our home, he insisted the kids and I come stay with him. Ivan lived a stone's throw away, and I was able to go back and forth to our unit, cleaning and doing a little packing every day.

The two things that made Ivan happy were his beer and his football. I made sure he always had them while I was staying there.

Living with Ivan was a blessing. I appreciated just having electricity again. There was hot water to warm up baby's bottle and the convenience of a hot shower, which sure beat travelling to caravan parks to sneak one.

I was really missing Mack, and with my two older kids at school all day, I spent a lot of time cleaning out our unit. Baby and I would leave in the morning and come back when school was out. This way Ivan had time to himself, and if people wanted to score, they would find me at the unit.

One morning as I was packing some stuff in our unit, an old acquaintance appeared at the front door. I was a little suspicious about how she knew where to find me. I had not seen her in a long time. She looked a little shaky when she asked me if I could score her some smack.

"I only have morph. One hundred milligrams for eighty bucks," I replied.

"Cool," she said, handing me the money.

While she mixed her shot, she told me how she'd been living with some guy who'd been selling speed and who'd been harassed by some bikies. She said the following day, when she returned home from scoring, she found the guy hanging by a rope behind his bedroom door.

"What's this guy's name?" I asked, freaking out.

"Snake," she replied.

"You've got to be joking!" I said, in shock and disbelief.

Something was very fishy about her story.

If it were true, what motive was there for his death, and why hadn't we heard about it on the news? I was still waiting on news about his interrogation, and this bit of information just added to my frustration.

There was never a day that I did not wonder about Snake. It had been eighteen months since I had reported him, and until now there had been no more news flashes and nothing more said about the killer. It all seemed very strange. At times I got angry and rang the number again to find out what was going on, but they never gave me any answers.

After she left, I went back to Ivan. He was always watching the telly, so I asked him to keep his eyes and ears open for any news flashes of a murder. From what I could tell, there was nothing in the papers or in the news about a murder or suicide. It was all very odd, and despite asking around, no one could tell me where Snake had gone.

A week later Mack was released from jail. After scoring morph, we returned to Ivan's house. We could tell Ivan was asleep because he was snoring heavily. So heavily that he could not hear us knocking, even though we knocked so hard we woke the entire neighbourhood.

Finally, due to our persistent knocking, Ivan heard us, got up, and answered the door. He seemed very heavy on his feet. Without warning, Ivan suddenly dropped to his knees and fell over backward.

I freaked out and shouted, "Help! What's wrong with him?"

Ivan's eyes were wide open, but he was not breathing. I yelled out to Mack to check his pulse. He could not find one.

I panicked and ran next door to call an ambulance. When they finally arrived, they removed his shirt and discovered he had previously suffered a serious heart condition, judging by the huge scar on his chest. While the ambulance officer tried to resuscitate him, I was praying aloud, asking God to help Ivan, but it was no good.

"Sorry, he's gone," the ambulance officer said.

I watched through tear-filled eyes as they closed his eyelids. My focus then turned to my children, who were looking on. This wonderful, caring person who had helped us in a time of need had just died right in front of them.

After they took him away, we knew we could not remain in his apartment. We helplessly gathered our things and went in search of a place to stay. It was ten thirty. All of us were very shaken by Ivan's death.

We decided to visit our morph dealer. He and his wife lived by themselves in a really big house. They were a lovely couple. Bruno was Italian and his wife was Indigenous. After hearing about our ordeal, they offered to let us stay in their home.

It was very convenient living with our dealer, as the stuff was right there, no need to go running anywhere. However, when Bruno's supply ran out, as it sometimes did, we would have to travel long distances to get the pills. This was a pain because most days we were both sick and hanging out. Bruno was okay because he could get morphine ampoules straight from his doctor, but he would never in a million years share them. He needed to make them last until his script for morphine was due.

One morning we were both very sick, and Mack had to go stealing in that condition. He thought a brand-name toolbox would get us out of trouble. Going to the closest hardware store was very risky, as he had done it several times before, but he went anyway.

"Please hurry, babe," I said, squirming in my bed of pain.

Hours went by, and I wondered what was taking so long. Before I knew it, it was dark outside and it was going on seven o'clock. Then I heard the house phone ring. It was Mack calling from lock-up. He had been charged with stealing again.

It felt like there was no end to the misery I was living. I was so over it and found myself getting angry with God. For a long time I had been waiting for God to answer my prayers and save me from my miserable life. I did not want to live this way. I would frequently cry out, "I believe in you, so why am I still living this way?"

However, there was no answer, and as I lay in bed, rolled up tightly in my sweat-soaked sheets, Bruno came to my rescue, handing me two over-the-counter painkillers.

"Sorry, Angel, this is all I can do."

Yeah, right, I thought, knowing he could have given me some of his ampoule. Even a skerrick of it would have been enough to ease my pain and he knew it.

I sat up in bed shivering. I carefully broke one of the tablets in half. I had to make them last as I did not know when I would be getting my next hit. I knew that half a tablet would only be enough to take a slight edge off the pain, but it turned out to be enough. I fell asleep for a few hours, only to wake up in the horrors again.

Through all of this, my poor kids were left to fend for themselves.

When Steele saw how sick I was, he called his sister, and together they helped me out of bed, leading me outside by the arms. I sat in the sunshine while I sipped on a hot cup of coffee little Carina had made.

Bruno and his wife were also out there having a cuppa and soaking up the warm morning sun. Bruno looked up at me with a half-sorry look on his face and handed me a slip of paper. "If you really want to leave and go back east, then here's your opportunity."

"What is it?" I asked and then realized the slip of paper he had handed me was a check.

The check was a computer printout made out to "account payee only." The address on the check showed that it was Bruno's neighbour, who was away overseas. Bruno explained that I needed to gently and carefully scrape off the word "only" with a safety pin so it said "account payee," and then deposit it into an account that I had access too.

I had never done anything like this before, and I was not real sure it was going to work, but I sure as hell was keen to give it a try, as the check was for a staggering $5,000, more than enough to cover the costs of moving back east.

For This Cause

That day I went to see an old friend to borrow some clothes so I could portray myself as the account holder of the check. I put on a white floral blouse and a long black skirt. This could very well incriminate me, but as Chopper Reid had often said, "You can't let the truth get in the way of a good yarn!" This was so true. Nervously I got dressed thinking that if this failed, they would lock me up immediately.

So far the easy part was over, and amazingly, the needle-scratching technique worked. Now I was psyching myself up to walk into a bank somewhere. I carefully chose one and walked in. There was no one inside apart from the one young woman behind the counter looking eager to serve me.

"Can I help you?" she asked.

I put on my mature voice and said, "I would like to put this check into this account please. This is my son's account. He's on his honeymoon and I'd like to surprise him. How long will it be until it clears?"

To my surprise, she took the check, along with the bit of paper with the account details on it, and vigorously typed away. She then slid the check back to me face down and asked me to sign. I carefully signed the name on the check and handed it back to her.

"All done! It will clear in five working days," she said. "Will that be all?"

"Yes, thank you very much," I replied and left.

As I walked out, it dawned on me that I had successfully deposited the check into Mack's account. If it cleared, it was our ticket out of this mess.

Now all I needed to do was get Mack out of jail so he could withdraw the money. I got busy planning our escape, as I had a feeling the check would clear.

I thought I should ring my mum and let her know my plans. When I did, my little sister, Gianna, answered the phone and told me Mum and Dad were in Italy and were not due back for a couple of weeks.

139

The next day Gianna came to visit me, and while we were sitting in her car chatting, I asked if she would help me. I explained that with Mum and Dad away in Italy, it was an ideal opportunity for her to help me off the heroin.

To my surprise, she shook her head no.

I started yelling. "What? You are family, and while Mum is away you *will* help me!"

She put the car in drive and started moving forward, a hint for me to get out. I did, all the while screaming at the top of my lungs. "You wonder why I never change. You're never there for me. I disown you and never want to see your face again!"

I slammed the passenger door. She sped off, looking back at me in her rear-view mirror. I stood in the middle of the road, tears streaming down my face as I watched her drive away. I wondered if she even cared.

Deep down I did not blame her for not wanting to help. Months ago, I had robbed the family's house and stolen $350 of Gianna's savings. She probably feared in her heart that I would do it again. This thought settled me a little, but I was still bitter inside. I felt that if only my family was prepared to take the risk and help me, I might just be able to turn my life round.

The next morning I was sitting in the sun with a cup of hot coffee, thinking about how I could get Mack out of jail. A red car pulled in to the driveway. It was Gianna! After yesterday's episode, I had not thought I would see her so soon, if at all. I walked over to her and was surprised when she asked me if I wanted to come home with her.

"Are you sure?" I asked.

"Round the kids up and get in," she said.

As we drove back to my parents' place, she glanced at me fearlessly in the rear-view mirror. I admired her courage in giving me a second chance.

As I entered the family home, it felt cold without my mother, who was always cooking. She was the master chef of the family, and the aroma of Italian cuisine was the "red carpet" of our home. The house felt extremely cold, and physically, I did too.

By this time, the last of the painkillers was wearing off. I was breaking out in hot and cold sweats. I reached for my jumper and some tissues as my nose began running uncontrollably. Then a wave of aches and pains came crashing down on me, making it hard to stand. I reached for a chair and braced myself as the pain of withdrawal took over.

Gianna stared in disbelief as she tried to comprehend what was happening. She rushed to Mum's medicine cupboard, pulling out a large box of Mum's pills, asking if there was anything in it that would help me feel better.

"Are there any of those painkillers?" I asked.

She fumbled through the box, eventually handing me a box of non-addictive painkillers, which Mum used for severe back pain—the pain Mum claimed I had caused her through my birth.

"Here, drink this' it will warm you up," Gianna said.

I popped a painkiller, chasing it down with the glass of straight whisky, which she gave me.

My little sister, a qualified hairdresser, decided it was a good time to pamper me with a haircut while I sat there helpless, sipping on my glass of whisky. My hair had not been cut for years, and who knows, it was probably contributing to the heavy weight I was feeling right then. Half an hour later I started to feel better—not 100 percent but enough to go out and grab pizza and videos for a relaxing evening together.

The next morning when I woke up, Gianna was saying good-bye as she left for work. I started to get up so we could leave with her, but as I pulled the blankets off, she insisted it was okay and told me to stay. That afternoon when Gianna returned home from work, we sat and talked over coffee. After I finished praising her for what she had already done, I hit her with the big question.

"Sis, I know how much of an ask this has been already, but it's not complete unless Mack gets out of jail. I guess I'm begging you to bail Mack out of jail so he can do the detox program with me."

She stared at me and for a minute. There was silence.

"Are you kidding—what if he jumps bail? I'm then up for $3,000!"

I spent the entire evening assuring her that would not happen. Gianna was not convinced about my big story that all would be okay, but she could see how desperate I was. After I went for a consultation at the detox clinic, she was convinced that I was serious about getting off the drugs. Two days later, she bailed Mack out of jail.

Driving home from the jail that day, I could not wait to get Mack alone so I could tell him about the check. When we were finally alone, the first thing he asked for was a shot. While Gianna ducked out to the shops, I gave him some money to race round to our dealer on the next street. (In the last week leading up to our detox treatment, we used heavily.)

After Gianna left for work the next morning, I asked Mack to ring the bank to see if the check had cleared.

He nodded while still on the phone.

"Quick, let's go get it out!" I yelled.

We ran back in to the kitchen to ask Gianna's boyfriend for a lift to the bank. I was so excited because this meant we could finally head back east.

Mack went into the bank while I watched nervously from the passenger seat of the car. Just as I was thinking he was taking his time, out walked Mack with a great big grin on his face and a spring in his step. He jumped into the car flashing a wad of hundred-dollar bills, $5,000 worth of them!

We threw a bill on Gianna's boyfriend's lap and asked him to drive us to the nearest travel agent. It was so funny because he did not know what was going on, and for all he knew we could have just robbed the bank.

We were ecstatic, and I felt as though my prayers had been answered.

After booking our tickets, I then had to tell Gianna that we were leaving, hoping she would not freak out about the surety on Mack's bail. She did just that—freaked out!

"You can't!" she insisted.

I explained, telling her, "I have to and when I go, you need to ring the cops. Ask them to revoke the bail because we're not complying with your conditions. They will then issue a warrant for our arrest." (This had been the case once before, when another lady had me on bail. The police had removed the bail and then come to get me. I figured it would work in this instance as well.)

My sister was not convinced but I kept reassuring her.

CHAPTER THIRTEEN

August 2002 Detox

It was to be our last day addicted to heroin. Tomorrow we would be off to a rehabilitation centre to undergo a rapid detox program. Mack bought a full box of morph. We hit that box hard, knowing it was our last. My little sister knew exactly what we were doing. She said nothing, but her silence spoke volumes. When she left the house, she took the kids with her so they would not be around us.

Heavily stoned, I sought God and began to write down my prayer to Him.

Diary Entry, August 6, 2002

"Dear God, tomorrow is the big day. Help me. Give us both strength and courage to go through with the detox and help us break free from this disgusting habit that belongs only to Satan himself. I want to live for you, Lord! In Jesus's name I pray, amen."

The following morning when I woke up, I checked the time. It was still early, so I snuggled back up to Mack while I watched baby Storm sleeping in her portable cot. Then I saw Gianna peering through the door that was slightly open. Being careful not to wake baby up and unsure of how I would respond, she whispered, "Are you going?"

I smiled and nodded.

A look of relief came over her face.

At our appointment the day before, the nurse had given Mack and me strict orders *not* to use any drugs within the twenty-four hours prior to commencing treatment, as it was dangerous to do so. I ignored these orders when Mack passed me a syringe full of morph. As I strapped up my arm, I prayed, "This is it, Lord. Lead me to the detox centre."

On our way to the clinic, I asked Gianna if she was going to be all right with the kids. She was a wonderful aunty, and I wanted to let her know how much I appreciated her taking a few days off work to help us. I hugged my kids good-bye and asked them to look after Aunty Lulu (as they called her).

Once inside the detox centre I was taken to a room where a man was seated at a desk. He introduced himself as a psychiatrist. He was eager to ask me questions such as how much and how frequently I used, so they would know how much of a specific medication to give me. It would also help them determine what sort of medication I would take after the surgery. This would be antipsychotic medication to help with depression, plus sedatives and sleepers to help with the effects of the treatment.

The treatment involved using a specific drug that would block the part of the brain that feels pleasure when alcohol or any sort of narcotic is used. When this part of the brain is blocked, the need to use heroin is blocked as well, making it easier to stop using. Special implants, about nine mm. in diameter and about 1.9 cm. in length are inserted under the skin through a one-inch incision in the lower abdomen.

After seeing the shrink, I was taken to a huge room where a nurse was laying plastic-covered foam mattresses on the floor. As I was waiting to be admitted to the surgery room, the door opened and a girl came out with the help of two nurses. They lay her down and covered her with blankets.

As I watched, I thought, *Okay, this looks easy. I can do this,* and I became eager to start the treatment. All of a sudden the girl woke up screaming, thrashing around on her mattress.

"What's wrong with her?" I asked the nurse, who was rushing to the girl's aid, a huge syringe in her hand.

"She is withdrawing, caused by the medication we gave her."

It was explained that the medication being used was a drug that reverses the effects of heroin overdose. It makes you go straight into a withdrawal state by stripping the opioids out of the opioid receptors in the brain.

After the small implants have been inserted, the body is flushed through an IV connection into a vein. It takes five to seven hours for the whole detox process. I can tell you that the whole experience is *extremely* unpleasant. The withdrawal symptoms include body aches and pains, diarrhoea, increased heart rate, fever, sweating, nausea, weakness, irritability, and trembling, and all of these symptoms are usually present *all at once*. It really is pretty bad—but it is better than dying.

By now the nurse had noticed the look of sheer horror on my face, but she assured me all would be okay. I was sceptical after watching this poor girl in her delirious state, running into the padded walls. The nurses helped her back to bed, but she got up and did it all again. For a split second I thought of leaving, walking straight out of there. Luckily, Mack was in with the psychiatrist at that time, otherwise he would have up and left for sure.

Despite how I was feeling, I knew deep down that I had to stay. I began to draw strength and courage from God, drawing near to Him in prayer.

I heard the nurse repeat once more that everything would be okay. She handed me a handful of tablets, most of them antibiotics, to prevent infection occurring after the surgery. Right after I took the tablets, she took my blood pressure and pulse before leading me into the theatre room and onto an operating table, where a famous medical professional looked down at me through his Coke-bottle glasses.

With a big smile, he said hi and told me he was going to give me some "happy juice," instructing me to start counting backward from ten.

"Ten, 9, 8 …"

Only God knows what happened next. I remember waking up with severe pain and feeling horribly groggy from the anaesthetic. I sat up with the help of nurses who were trying to stop me from ripping out the cannula (a tube hospitals use to help deliver fluids into the body) hanging out of my ankle. I felt it there, and it was annoying me. I was then brought to the same room as earlier. This time the other girl was sleeping soundly.

Once on the bed, I started hallucinating about blocks of heroin. It was like a dream where I was trying to use the drug but was unable. I remember howling and squirming, rolling about, getting up, and throwing myself back down. It was sheer hell!

The nurses came over to me, one telling the other that I needed more of something because my reaction was so severe. I realized it probably had not helped that I had had my last shot of morphine only an hour before we arrived at the clinic. I began to understand how highly dangerous it was to do that when undergoing this sort of treatment.

The next thing I remember was the nurses giving me some relief through the IV tube that I was still trying to rip out of my ankle. The pain was *extremely* intense. I made the desperate determined decision to ride it out by sheer willpower and pleaded with God to give me relief through it all.

At one stage, I got up and sat on a chair. From where I was sitting, I could see Mack lying on a mattress with a blanket on him. I remember thinking how sedated I was because I was finding it difficult to focus on him.

Suddenly Mack sat up and started groping the end of his mattress, trying to rip it apart. I realized he must have started hallucinating blocks of heroin as well. It was quite funny to watch. Even in the middle of my pain, I found laughter as I watched him desperately trying to rip his mattress apart for what was not there.

With each passing hour, the nurses came and injected me with more medication and sedatives until I felt less and less irritable and drifted in and out of sleep. I thought I must be getting closer to the end of the pain threshold; it was now bearable, as far as "bearable" goes. I remember waking up properly at last—and to my surprise feeling no pain at all. It was finally over. A nurse approached, sat me up, and gave me a glass of water.

"How are you feeling, love?" she asked.

Amazingly, I felt no pain. It had finally subsided, but I still felt heavily sedated. They helped me up onto a chair, and I noticed the clock on the wall read 4:55. After drinking the water, I spent the remaining thirty-five minutes trying to sober up from the sedation. Gianna was coming to pick me up and would have the children with her, so I had to be alert and fully functioning because my children were going to need me. Mack was half an hour behind me in the program. We could see each other but were not able to communicate. While I sat there, my mind wandered off, seeking God.

I cannot explain why or how, but I could always feel when God was around me. His presence seemed to have a way of getting my attention, and I constantly thought about Him.

God was always in my heart, and I was always involving Him in my situations. I do not know why, but nothing grabbed my attention more than the presence of God in my life. However, I could not understand it. I was living contrary to what I had been taught about God's righteousness and goodness. I was living in sin, one sin after the other, yet here was this amazing feeling of love and acceptance, which I knew without a doubt was God Himself.

By the time my sister arrived I could stand but needed something to hold onto. I felt it was the worst day of my life but at the same time the most important day because it was the beginning of a completely new chapter.

During my time of seeking God after the operation, He showed me a timeline on the road to recovery. The road was long and rugged, but He showed me that with His help, I would get through it. I was given a vision of a little child holding onto her father's hand as they walked along together. The child was stumbling over rocks and rubble while she held tightly to her father. This picture gave me great comfort. I knew I was that little child, and if I just held onto Gods hand, I would make it.

For one week Mack and I were gravely sick and bedridden. To my embarrassment, I even soiled my bed. We had not expected it to be this bad. My sister had no choice but to stay home from work and nurse us to better health. I am forever in her debt.

By the second week all the bad symptoms were gone, but I felt weak and lethargic, with no energy to do my daily chores. My sister had to go back to work, and that's when I asked Mack to go score a gram of speed so I could feel better. I did not want to take it but felt I needed it, as Mum and Dad were due back from Italy the following day. I wanted to have energy for the remaining time we had left together.

Right after taking the speed, conviction covered me like a thick blanket until I repented by scribbling in my diary. "Dear God, please forgive me. I feel like crap and can't believe I'm using this shit to feel better."

I do not know how to explain this, but somehow I felt as though God understood. I felt loved by Him despite my weakness to drugs. The truth was, part of me still wanted the drugs. That feeling was not going away in a hurry because for most of my life, drugs had been my companion and escape from the reality of my hurts and my life.

I needed something else to replace them. I did not know how I was going to do it, but I knew this was going to be the new challenge that I would face in the very near future. Deep down I truly did have a burning desire to ditch them all.

When Mum and Dad arrived home, they were very happy to hear of our recovery. Then sadness came over me when I realized

I was leaving my family again. I retreated to my room, teary-eyed, and wrote in my diary once more.

"Dear God, we are leaving soon. Thank You for all You have done. Be with my sister when she finds out she has to pay for Mack's bail and help us to return it to her as soon as possible. I am sad to leave my family behind. Please be with Mum and Dad, but most of all, be with us as we leave this life of tragedy behind and begin our journey to freedom from all drugs and a better future. Love you, Lord. In Jesus's name I pray, amen."

The night of August 27, 2002, was a sad night. We were unhappy to be leaving but felt we had no choice. We were also leaving a trail of chaos behind us.

We were both wanted for questioning and for many offences ranging from theft to federal fraud. We had been pinching script books from doctors' desks and writing out hundreds of scripts for morphine. All these offences were indictable, meaning that if apprehended at this stage, there would be no point in leaving, for they would have the power to extradite us back, effectively ruining our chances of starting a new life.

Our flight was due to take off at ten thirty. The time came to say farewell. My heart ached as I watched Mum embrace her eight-month-old granddaughter. Tears flowed as I walked quickly to the plane, constantly turning to look back and wave. Mack and the kids followed close behind. As I walked, I felt those steps of sorrow turning to leaps of joy—God's presence was walking with me.

Shortly after takeoff the kids made the most of their time by watching a movie that was screening. I went off in to my own little world, thanking God for getting us out on time. I was also reflecting on my life and all I was leaving behind. My past flashed before my eyes, including the unsolved mystery of Snake and the possibility he was the serial killer. I thought how suspicious it was, that nothing had resulted from the investigation or from the report I had made. Had there been foul play, or was someone protecting him? I didn't feel safe, knowing what I did.

Our aircraft finally deposited us back on the East Coast, and we boarded a coach for the last leg of our journey to the country town where they were living. It was winter, and when we arrived at our destination, I noted the blanket of ice covering the ground. I remember thinking, *What a terrible place to come and dry out in!* (One of the main symptoms of withdrawal is the feeling of being cold all the time.)

The good thing about being back was that Baron and I were finally reunited. There were tears of joy as we embraced after the nine long months apart.

"I'm so glad you're here, Mum. I didn't think you'd ever come. It's a miracle," he cried.

"Me too, mate; me too." I held him tight, realizing how much he had missed us.

We were staying at the home of Mack's mum. She was away on holidays for another two weeks, which meant we had her bedroom and full reign of the house. Ziggy was also staying at Mum's. I thought he was looking a little rough around the edges but nothing a shower couldn't fix.

Our first morning was spent huddled around the gas heater. It was absolutely freezing, and there was no relief from the frosty morning air. The day eventually warmed up, and we were able to catch up with the rest of the family over a barbecue lunch, where we watched the kids playing happily, reunited with their big brother, Baron.

On the second day I woke up feeling very ill. The amphetamines had worn off, and I was battling, trying to find enough energy just to get out of bed. After having some coffee, I sorted out the kids' school enrolments. I did not know how I was going to cope, feeling the way I did. Then I remembered God had shown me a timeline of how long and rough it would be. I knew I had to ride this one out, allowing for God's timing in the healing process.

Three days passed. Ordinary time was definitely not on my side, and country life took a bit of getting used to. We had shifted from living a fast-paced city life to a painfully slow country lifestyle where days felt like weeks, months, or at times years. Mack's younger brother, Blue, got tired of seeing us in our sick bed every day and thought we could do with some help.

"You fellas look like you could do with a pickup," he said. My eyes lit up.

"Can you get some speed, boy?"

"Yeah." He nodded.

"Then go get some, Blue," I said, handing him a hundred-dollar bill.

A week passed by. Scoring drugs in a country town was not that easy. There was a lot of messing around, and we had to wait for days, which made me anxious. When Blue finally got hold of some speed, the quality was poor compared to in the city. Nevertheless, it took away the sick feeling and got me out of bed to do some much-needed chores around the house. It was a break from feeling sick every day.

We had been there ten days, and Mack and I were desperate to feel better. Unfortunately, the speed Blue had been able to acquire reversed what little healing we had gained.

We decided to go doctor shopping for drugs known as benzodiazepines. These drugs were administered in jails, within the first five days of incarceration, to inmates with severe alcohol or drug addiction. The drugs helped with withdrawal.

The only problem with these tablets was that Mack and I would take the whole bottle instead of the prescribed dose. To make matters worse, I would drink three bottles of red wine on top of them. This mix of drugs and alcohol barely affected me because I still had a very high tolerance to heroin.

As bad as I felt doing all this, I felt I needed it, and as I drew nearer to God in repentance, He reassured me, saying, "It's okay. One by one they'll go, and together we will conquer them all."

I trusted God in His wise counsel; it was all I had. He knew my heart, and that mattered more to God. I had found over time that God was not looking at my actions as much as He was looking at the *reactions* and *thoughts* of my heart.

I had to face up to the fact that heroin was a very big thing in my life—a thing that had nearly killed me. There was no way the drugs could be knocked on the head at once. Breaking free of them was going to take time and a strong, steady commitment.

Two weeks on, Mack's mum finally arrived home from her holiday. She was very shocked to see us looking so sickly but very happy to have her son back after eight long years of separation.

It was good to be together again, but with Mum back, the house felt a little crowded. It was time to start looking for a place of our own. This had to be done on foot as we had no means of transport, and no one in the family was offering any help. Despite still being sick, I continued to take speed for the energy.

Finally, after many knock-backs, a cosy three-bedroom house was found. It was within walking distance of the town centre.

Diary Entry

"Dear God, thank you for what you've done so far. I have been off heroin for six months now. My eyes are starting to open, and for the first time I'm seeing that my children are running amuck because my parenting skills are bad and are in need of a major brush up. Please help me, Lord. My life is a mess, and I'm hanging onto You. I might not be doing heroin but I'm still taking drugs in other forms. Please help me break these habits. I desire to live for you. *Help!* In Jesus's name I pray. Amen."

It was not long before we knew our way around town. As we settled into the country town lifestyle, it seemed the only people we attracted were others like ourselves, giving us more access to buy and use drugs.

From week to week we struggled, with no money for the barest essentials. A charity organization became our only hope, giving us food vouchers for a diet consisting of bread, eggs, and processed meat rolls.

Deep down I was unhappy with the way things were going in my life. Our move back east had been made with the intention of changing things for the better, but the dream of becoming clean seemed way beyond my grasp. In desperation I sought God for answers.

Some days He answered with clear instructions, while other days He would seemed distant, not saying anything.

One day I was sitting on my back steps overlooking town and thinking how there had to be more to this miserable, meaningless life. If I gave up the drugs, there still wasn't any reason to live it, even if I were straight. Suddenly, a flock of birds flew playfully in the sky right in front of me, surprising me. As I watched, they appeared to form an image of a couple dancing in the sky. I was in awe and thought, *This must be God.* My spirit rose from the depths of despair to a place of unbelievable tranquillity. There was no doubt in my heart that this amazing display had been an act of God.

Back in the real world, Mack and I realized we could not keep buying little costly packets of speed. We decided it was time to start doing what we knew how to do best. If we were going to use, we needed to sell. We started making runs to the nearest city to pick up better-quality drugs, cutting out the middleman, so to speak.

During our trips, I noticed certain cars following us, but I just shrugged it off as paranoia. Then one day while we were on our way home from one of our runs, I noticed a motorcycle following us. The rider was dressed completely in black leather and was riding a black motorbike. He followed us from our dealer's house to the outskirts of the city. I began to feel paranoid, to the point where I slid down in the passenger seat so my head was not visible. Blue was driving at the time, and I asked him to take a left detour onto a gravel road, to see if the motorcyclist was really following us. As we turned off, the bike turned off too.

It was not an easy road for a motorbike to travel on with all its bends and potholes. I asked Blue to stop at a rest area to see what the biker would do next. When he did, the biker slowed down, proceeded a little further, and then turned round and went very slowly past us.

Mack was getting cranky, thinking I was hallucinating from my addiction, but the truth was, the biker *was* following us. The next question was, what did he want? I became irritable, felt scared and very much on my own, because everyone around me thought I was going mad. Then my fear turned to anger as I thought of the injustice with the serial killer. Enough was enough! I deliberately eyed the bike rider aggressively. I wanted to let him know I was aware of him and that I had witnesses around me, such as the people at the rest area who were taking a lunch break. I decided not to move from the rest area until he was gone.

This was just one of many odd, unexplainable incidences that occurred.

Another example happened two days later, when Mack and I were invited to his sister's house for a roast dinner. I was asked to set the table in the dining room, while baby Storm played with her aunty in the lounge room. The dining room was very dark. Even switching on the light seemed to make no difference. The boyfriend of Mack's sister walked over to the window, pulled open the heavy curtains, and then left the room again. I was captivated by the view. I had never seen these curtains opened before, and I gazed out to where the mountains met the skyline.

Suddenly a red laser beam appeared, moving through the glass window. I dropped to the floor and began to weep bitterly, totally scared and confused. It seemed like only seconds had passed before

I heard something like a Harley Davidson start up, in the direction from which the laser beam had come. After hearing it drive away, I crawled on my knees back to the lounge room, found my baby girl, and hugged her tight.

The strangest thing was that nobody asked me what I was doing, crying and crawling on the floor. However, when Mack's sister saw how scared I was, she started crying too. I wondered why on earth *she* was crying. Did she know something I didn't? Such as the reason I just saw a laser beam come at me through the dining room window? Was someone out to kill me? If so, why didn't he just walk in and do it?

None of it was making any sense. In my mind, I questioned whether the rest of the family knew anything about it.

After this, I felt like someone was stalking me, but nobody would believe me. Why would they?

Then it happened again.

Something like a red laser beam came through the front bedroom window while I was fixing my hair in front of the mirror. Once again I dropped to the floor, crawling to a corner of the room where I sat, terrified, quietly crying to God.

As I sat there, I spotted a Bible among some books scattered on the floor. Longing for comfort, I grabbed it and opened it. It opened up at Psalm 6.

> Lord, do not rebuke me in Your anger or discipline me in Your wrath.
>
> Have mercy on me, LORD, for I am faint; heal me, LORD, for my bones are in agony.
>
> My soul is in deep anguish. How long, LORD, how long?
>
> Turn, LORD, and deliver me; save me because of Your unfailing love.
>
> Among the dead, no one proclaims Your name. Who praises You from the grave?

I am worn out from my groaning.

All night long I flood my bed with weeping and drench my couch with tears.

My eyes grow weak with sorrow; they fail because of all my foes.

Away from me, all who do evil, for the LORD has heard my weeping.

The LORD has heard my cry for mercy; the LORD accepts my prayer.

All my enemies will be overwhelmed with shame and anguish; they will turn back and suddenly be put to shame. (Psalm 6 NIV)

Wow. The words were so personal and relevant to what I was going through. *How can this be?* I thought before wondering, *What else is in this book?*

I had always thought the Bible merely contained stories of Jesus, like the ones you learn in Sunday school. I had never read anything like Psalm 6 before. From this point, I kept my Bible close.

I sensed strongly that I was in danger. If someone was trying to kill me, what was his or her motive?

Now living in fear for my life, I became paranoid and aggressive toward everyone around me. I suspected my in-laws knew something. I felt I could not go to the cops. I had lost all faith in them after not getting anywhere in the matter of Snake. There was no one I could turn to—no one except God.

I was petrified to walk down town to get groceries in case someone was planning to shoot me. I prayed, asking God to protect me. Right after this, an idea came to mind—a smart idea at that. I decided to play a little game, calling a bluff on those people I believed were following me and stalking me at night.

My idea was to make out I had a hearing piece attached to my ear. I would touch my ear from time to time, pretending I was trying to hear someone talking to me. I would make signs with my fingers, as if I was making signals to someone else—someone who was monitoring me while watching for anyone else who might be keeping me under surveillance. I wanted it to look like I was wearing a wire and was being monitored by the cops. It must have worked because there were no more laser beam incidences, which was a great relief.

To look at me during this particular time would have been to look upon hostility. I was in a spiritual battle, a battle in which Satan wanted me dead.

CHAPTER FOURTEEN

Love and Acceptance

Days later, I met Blue's girlfriend, Bianca. Blue and Bianca had been separated for a few months, but then they began seeing each other again. Bianca and I hit it off when she began talking about her love for God. *Any friend of God's is a friend of mine,* I thought.

She was always boasting about the church she attended. She wanted us to go along one Sunday and meet the people, people who prayed for us even though we were still on heroin. The ironic thing was that while she was praying for us, she was living the tormented life of addiction herself.

I couldn't quite put my finger on what she thought I was going to get out of going to church, seeing as she was still on drugs as well. Nonetheless, she went to church every Sunday, and I have to admit I was getting a little curious about her church. In my case, sin had me running *from* church, not *to* it. One Sunday morning I decided to go along, no matter how my sinful life felt about it.

When I arrived, I was puzzled at their definition of church. I thought it all very strange. The church was located inside a centre for the elderly and was made up of a small group of about twenty-five people. When Bianca saw me standing by the entrance, she took me by the hand and introduced me to the senior pastor and his wife. They told me they had heard a lot about me and were very glad to meet me. Both of them made me feel very welcome.

The atmosphere in the church was warm, and so were the people. They had a four-person band to worship God, and the music touched my heart so deeply, I began to cry. I could not explain what I was feeling, but I believe it was God's Spirit touching mine. I began to feel at peace within myself, as though God was lifting the crippling weight of guilt and shame that I had been carrying around for so many years.

There was something inspiring and supernatural in being among others who were there for the same God—the God who had been following me around all my life. I felt like I was home.

These things were new to me. I had never seen this kind of worship before. People were crying aloud in prayer, lifting their hands up towards heaven and giving God praise. I could sense His Spirit like never before. The same presence that surrounded me when I was alone or sad was there in their praises.

"Wow, this is amazing!" I cried. "My God is here, and He is enjoying the praises of His people."

After the service, they put on a fantastic morning tea where we could all enjoy fellowship together. I met the rest of the church family—a very warm bunch of people who were not fazed at all when I went outside the building to smoke. In fact, there were others smoking out there as well. I was waiting for someone to come and tell us all off, but nothing like that happened, which I thought was incredible.

I had never experienced love and acceptance like I did that day at church. There was something very different about their God, and I felt very drawn to it all. The God of my childhood was portrayed as a big, mean, angry tyrant with a big stick, ready to whack me each time I did something wrong. However, with the recent events in my life, I was finding this portrayal to be false—even more so after attending Bianca's church.

A Monday morning came, and the kids left for school on the bus. Mack and his brothers were smoking their first session for the day. Suddenly there was a knock at the back door. When I opened it, smoke from the bong billowed out the door, right into the faces of two cranky real-estate women, who had come to see why we were behind in the rent. All I could do was hang my head in shame, knowing this was enough for an eviction notice.

"I'll have three weeks' rent for you next week, okay?" I promised before they turned and left.

"Great! We're going to be evicted over that, I just know it," I cried to nobody in particular.

Mack immediately offered me a bong, which I smoked. After that I withdrew from everyone to the back steps, wanting very badly to hear from God. I still believed He had the answers to all my problems.

A week after fixing the rent I was not surprised when we got an eviction notice served on us. Suddenly I was having déjà vu.

"Why?" I cried. "Why won't you help me, God? I believe in you. Why am I still in this mess? Why am I still making the same mistakes and never learning?"

It was as if I was expecting God to wave a magic wand and I would be changed, or taken out of the situation. Like a never-ending circle, my spirit was willing to change, but my flesh was too weak to follow.

I was desperately tired of repeatedly making the same mistakes, so I made the decision to give one of my addictions the flick. I figured the dope would be a good start. I did not go much on dope anyway, and it was causing most of the depression. I just needed to do *something*, for we were on the brink of becoming homeless yet again.

A court-ordered eviction was due any day now, as we had been squatting in our house for weeks, without paying any rent. Thankfully, a chick named Kelly, who would often score from us, offered us a place to stay. Unfortunately, that only lasted a week. Kelly and I broke out into a punch-up when I found out she had a thing for my Mack, and I swear she was trying to poison me. The six of us left, fleeing on foot, taking nothing more than baby's bag and pram.

We walked aimlessly to the other side of town before realizing the home of Mack's little brother was not very far away. It was nine thirty on a Saturday night and I did not want to intrude, but Mack insisted we had no choice. When Bianca and Blue answered our knock, they welcomed us in to where they were having a few drinks. They were happy to have some company. After explaining why we were out so late, on foot with all the kids, they insisted we stay.

Later that evening, as I was making the bed, Bianca asked me if I would go to church with her in the morning.

"Sure, I'd like that," I responded.

The date was August 15, 2003. I was in church. During praise and worship, as I listened to the words of a song, I broke down crying. I realized I had been running for more than thirteen years of my life, running from a God I thought was angry with me.

At the end of the sermon, the senior pastor gave an altar call, giving us an opportunity to receive Jesus or recommit our lives to God. I went up to the front, bawling my eyes out. He laid hands on me and prayed, welcoming me into the family of God.

It was great! At the end of the service, the church handed us a food parcel to which the whole congregation had contributed. I was over the moon with their loving generosity. The senior pastor's wife dropped it off at Blue and Bianca's house, along with blankets, pillows, mattresses, sheets, and even a cot for Storm.

Through these acts of kindness, I began to see God for who He truly was—a loving, caring, merciful, and gracious God. He was providing for our every need, even to the point that when we were homeless, Bianca asked us to stay with her and Blue until we were on our feet again. The senior pastor's wife was also supportive, staying in constant contact with us throughout the week.

Every Sunday we found ourselves in church. Going to church gave me inner strength and power. Each time I heard a message spoken from God's Word, I was able to take the information home and apply it to my life, whatever the topic.

Now began the battle to give up drug number three, and I knew it was not going to be easy. So far it had been a month since I had touched any dope. Church was giving me a sense of purpose, a reason not to want drugs anymore. The more involved I became in the life of the church, the more I wanted off it all. I could not wait for Sundays to come round. That's when Bianca suggested I become a part of her life group.

Once a week, Blue and Bianca hosted a life group in their home. They were made up of people who regularly attended church. Each group got together once a week to pray and discuss what was preached on Sunday and how we could apply this information to our own lives. It was fun! I enjoyed talking about the things of God. I found getting together and doing this regularly was beneficial. I sensed a real family connection with my group beyond the normal Sunday celebration.

As time passed, my love for the senior pastor and his wife grew. I was sure I could confide in them, whatever my issues. At this stage, they did not know all there was to know about me, but I felt it was now time to tell the pastor's wife about my addiction to speed and my plan to get off it. I also knew that if I exposed it by telling someone, I would have more of a hope of succeeding, as this way others could pray for me and hold me accountable.

When I told her, she was very loving and supportive. I believed Bianca was also confiding in her about the same thing, but after she left that day, Bianca argued that I should not have said anything. I knew then that I had exposed Satan's scheme to keep my addiction a secret. From that day on, I prayed to God to help me, for I knew the battle would rage every payday when I had the money to score the drug. Payday could never come fast enough for us.

When the next payday arrived, I woke up and realized Mack and Blue had already left to go score. I tried to figure out how I was supposed to say no to a shot once they returned. I was exasperated because I knew living in the same environment with other users was not going to help. It became obvious that their drug taking was going to be an everyday occurrence, so one day I left in search of another place to stay.

It was obvious Mack was not willing to stop. I left him there while I went looking for Ziggy, who was living on the other side of town in a tiny one-bedroom flat. It was extremely small, but I didn't care. I knew he would say yes when I asked if we could move in with him. After all, I reasoned, I was the mother of his kids.

He was kind enough to give Mack and me his bedroom, while he settled for a mattress on the floor, under the kitchen table, with his dog, Mishka.

One week later I found I was pregnant with my fifth child. Here I was repeating history, taking drugs while I was pregnant. I was so desperate to beat my addiction; I made the determined decision to go to church every Sunday without fail.

Each Sunday I left church, taking with me another awesome teaching from the Holy Bible (also known as God's Word, the "sword of truth") to fight my enemy, Satan, who was continually laughing at me. This was very real. Each time I gave in to a shot, I heard Satan laughing, saying I would have to wait until next payday to resist him all over again—Ha! Ha! Ha!

Enraged by this, I raced to my Bible, trying to find the peace that had been stolen from me, pleading with God to help me win the fight. I felt more and more that being around people who used drugs was making it impossible for me to say no to them. I longed for a clean environment with no users around me. I figured that if I went into a rehabilitation centre, I would have a sure hope of giving up the drugs.

However, God had another way in mind. I believed He was calling me to do something greater—He wanted me to put my trust in Him; He alone wanted to be my Counsellor. I couldn't just up and leave, anyway, as I had children and no one I trusted to look after them.

God heard my plea and answered. I heard His wonderful, quiet voice inside my heart saying, *My child, if you do this amongst the drug users, you will never be tempted to touch it again.*

Wow! This made perfect sense, but how was it going to be done? There were days Mack and I vowed not to touch it, and the next thing, there were people offering it to us free. I needed so much to say no. I needed a breakthrough.

I persisted in prayer, asking for God's help. There were Sundays when I did not want to go to church and I would be so disappointed in myself. Yet I pressed on, grabbing myself by the scruff of the neck and making myself go.

One particular Sunday, the senior pastor preached a sermon about resisting the Devil and standing our ground. He shared a scripture from the book of James. "Submit yourselves, then, to God. Resist the devil, and he will flee from you" (James 4:7 NIV)

He then made this statement: "Let's draw a line in the sand and not cross over it."

It did not sound like much, but I knew God was speaking to me. The words gave me power. It was what I needed. I went home confessing those words repeatedly to myself and to whomever else was around.

"I'm not crossing the boundary anymore!" I kept repeating. I was determined to win, constantly meditating on James 4:7: "Submit yourselves, then, to God. Resist the devil, and he will flee from you."

The key here was (and is) resistance—I needed to *resist* the temptation. The opportunity to resist arrived the next payday.

As I stood in the main street, I spotted my drug dealer walking fast and headed my way. I took a strong, determined stance, feeling ready to fight this temptation head on. Looking the drug dealer straight in the eye I prayed, asking God to do something. When the drug dealer saw the "stay back" expression on my face, he stopped dead in his tracks. Lucky for him he got the message. He about-faced and walked away.

I had passed the test!

A wonderful exhilaration and sense of inner power filled me. It was so strong that it left me at a loss for words. I laughed joyfully in Satan's face as he fled from my presence like a balloon full of air when it is let go. He was not very happy.

From that day on, I felt *aggressive* toward the drug. It was my way of staying strong. For once in my life I felt as though I had control, and my faith took me to a new level of trust in Jesus.

By now I had fallen in love with Jesus, and He began to heal me of my past wounds. He was pouring His oil of love on my broken heart. For weeks I was breaking down, on my knees in church. I could not stop crying. Jesus was melting my bitter-cold heart, and I had no control over my emotions. All I knew was that I needed Jesus in my life and was grateful to have found Him.

I finally found my place in this world—home in the loving arms of my Saviour, Jesus, and His beloved church. Light dawned—the unexplainable presence that had surrounded me as a child was none other than the Holy Spirit Himself. The Holy Spirit is God. He's a Person, the third Person of the Godhead, and He is God on earth.

The Holy Spirit of God began to minister to me as I opened my heart more and more. Even though I still had urges to get on the drugs, I had Divine power to resist. God was replacing addiction to drugs with His love, forgiveness, mercy, and grace.

As He began healing my painful past, I felt as though I did not *need* drugs anymore. I felt loved, accepted, and worthy of all He had for me. The more I read my Bible, the more I learnt who I was in Christ Jesus. I was taking in the knowledge of God, and it was transforming me.

I found a brand-new identity in Him, and a sense of freedom from who I used to be. I was now free to simply be *me*.

Through reading the Bible, I discovered that I had a reason to live and a purpose for living—God had a plan for my life. The purpose for giving up the drugs was not so God would love me more but so I could be healthy and live to do the things God had planned for me.

"For I know the plans I have for you," declares the LORD, "plans to prosper you and not to harm you, plans to give you hope and a future" (Jeremiah 29:11 NIV).

We had been living in Ziggy's flat for a month when I realized our homelessness was due to the way I had been living. Now I was keen to live life God's way. My way had not worked until now.

My future was beginning to look brighter, and I could not stop praising God for all He had done for me so far.

One morning I felt prompted by the Spirit of God to apply for priority housing. Still feeling led, I sent a letter to our local member of Parliament, telling him of our life story and how desperate we were for accommodation. We were seven people living in a one-bedroom flat. Not only that, I was pregnant and just about to have our fifth child. I waited patiently, trusting in God and believing it was only a matter of time before we were given our own home.

The doors to our newly built local church were officially opened on March 14, 2004, after a long haul of hard work and team effort. It was a happy day to see the project finally finished to that stage. Situated on the lovely creek that runs through town, it was like no other building on earth as far as I was concerned—a beautiful place where we could all gather to worship God as well as being a great venue for all sorts of celebrations.

It was truly a time for new beginnings, and on April 26, I gave birth to a healthy baby girl. In the early morning after her birth, I went outside the hospital building to have a smoke. As I looked out across the beautiful landscape, a name for baby came to me. I saw that the clouds were in line with each other, reflecting colours of pink and purple.

"I will call her April Sky," I declared. Then I paused when I felt prompted to ask God for a name. "What will you call her, Lord?" I asked, not really expecting a reply.

"You can have Sky, but I call her J—,"the Spirit of God whispered.

I was surprised, as the name He gave me was not a name I liked very much. I was more into rare names that stuck out in the crowd. This name was not one of them. Amazingly, that name was later confirmed when a popular character in a children's movie came with a McDonald's kids meal that Bianca and Blue bought for the kids. To me, that in itself was confirmation from God.

Wow! I thought. *When God is asked, He* will *speak. That is truly a miracle.*

(As I write this book, I have just learnt that my daughter's name means Grace of God, which is what my story is all about.)

Exactly one month to the day, another miracle arrived in the form of a letter from government housing. The letter confirmed there was a house for us!

I could not believe it. I had phoned the week before, and they had said there was still nothing available. Collecting the key from the housing office, we went looking for the address.

I assumed it was in the government housing area of town, but we couldn't find it anywhere. We asked someone where it was, and they told us it was on the other side of town.

We finally found the house on the main drag that leads out of town. I had to rub my eyes and check to see that I had the address right. This house looked nothing like the house I was expecting.

"This can't be it," I said to Bianca.

"It must be," she replied.

I was expecting a little old fibro house, smack bang in the middle of the housing area, but this was much more. Overwhelmed with joy I walked toward the house, holding out the key.

Out of nowhere I heard a voice *thundering* in to my spirit, saying, *This is nothing compared to what I have for you.*

There was an instant sense of favour pouring all over me. "Favour" because I did not deserve this house. God obviously thought I did. I was in total awe of God and all He was doing.

I fell in love with the house and could not believe it was ours. It was a brick veneer with two levels, with established gardens at the front, and a huge backyard. It was empty, but a local charity came through with furniture. There were no floor coverings or curtains, but I was thankful to have our own place, and so were my kids, especially Baron. I sensed he was happy for the first time since I could remember, and I felt very blessed by God.

CHAPTER FIFTEEN

Blessings Flow

It was now two years since I'd had my last shot of heroin, one year since I'd smoked any dope, and five months since I'd had any speed.

Living life straight was fantastic. God had taken every desire to use drugs away, and I no longer depended on anything but God Himself. I could feel He was working a miracle in my life, which was going to speak volumes to the rest of the community. The way I saw it, God was exalting me by placing me in a house situated on the main road, where the whole town could see God transforming me.

I was filled with desire to fly and excel in life, and God was the source of all my desires. I wanted nothing else but what He wanted for me. In fact, I was so hungry for more of Him that I wanted to be baptized straight away. To our pastor's surprise I wanted to be baptized the same way that Jesus was—Him in the Jordan River and me in the town creek. It was looking good until the senior pastor advised me it would not be safe.

On November 21, 2004, I was baptized in a pool, with my church family as witnesses to my commitment. I wanted nothing more in life than to follow Jesus. When I came up out of the baptismal waters, I received the Holy Spirit and was given a powerful prophecy by one of our pastors, who prayed and proclaimed the words, "You are a light in the darkness." These seven words meant a lot, and I felt like a warrior equipped to take God's light into the darkest places—places from which I had recently emerged.

After being baptized, I also received the spiritual gift of tongues, which is a language that only God can understand. Now I was able to build myself up by praying in the Spirit during my prayer times and anytime I wanted.

I was so grateful that the Holy Spirit was with me, leading me to live an abundant and extraordinary life. I felt as though I had the power to live effortlessly in Christ Jesus because the evidence was that life was getting better, with the support of our church family.

The senior pastor's wife would pick us up every Sunday for church and drop us off afterward because we did not have a car.

My daily routine consisted of an early rise for a walk at five in the morning and then reading my Bible before anyone else was up. Each morning when I read from the Bible, God would reveal things to me about His values and principles and the conditions to receiving His promises that would enrich my life even more.

One Sunday morning the senior pastor preached about tithing, the sowing and reaping principle. He shared how God wants to bless his people financially.

> "Bring the whole tithe into the storehouse, that there may be food in my house. Test me in this," says the Lord Almighty, "and see if I will not throw open the floodgates of heaven and pour out so much blessing that there will not be room enough to store it. I will prevent pests from devouring your crops, and the vines in your fields will not drop their fruit before it is ripe," says the Lord Almighty. "Then all the nations will call you blessed, for yours will be a delightful land," says the Lord Almighty." (Malachi 3:10–13 NIV)

This scripture spoke volumes. It challenged me, to say the least. I went home that day praying and asking God to help me tithe, as I wanted to see the floodgates of heaven opening up in my life. However, I was also fearful that I wouldn't have enough money for our needs if I gave God 10 percent.

That week I was to receive $600, and 10 percent of that was $60. I wrote out my weekly budget. As it worked out, I was already short for the shopping, but I decided I was going to trust God. All over my budget I scribbled prayers that said, "Please help me tithe, Lord." At the top of my budget was my $60 for tithing.

The next day, when I left to go shopping, I felt confident that I would grab only the necessities. However, to my surprise, as I was withdrawing the cash from the ATM, there was an extra $175 in my account. What the!?

You can be sure that when God says, "Test me in this," He is going to prove himself.

As His promises manifested in my life, my faith grew. I was hungry for more of his Word (Bible), and I recalled a scripture that Jesus spoke concerning this: "Jesus answered, 'It is written: "Man shall not live on bread alone, but on every word that comes from the mouth of God"'" (Mathew 4:4 NIV).

I was living, that's for sure. God's word was alive and active in my world, and I wanted to see more of His promises come to light.

During this significant time in my life, God knew we needed a car. One afternoon it was announced on the news that the government wanted to pay families $600 per child—and I had five children. As if that was not enough, the government announced again in the budget that this time they wanted to give families a one-off, $1,000 payment for each child, as well as the $600. This was a staggering amount. Well and truly more than enough for the car we needed.

I had great plans for that money. I wanted to buy a car, lay down some floor covering on my bare concrete floors, and if I had some money left, buy a new bed because the one from the local charity had seen better days.

It was during this time that God also blessed me with a visit from my own mum. During her stay, she added her touch to the house, making it feel more like a home.

As I meditated on tithing promises, I realized God had more promises. "'I will prevent pests from devouring your crops, and the vines in your fields will not drop their fruit before it is ripe,' says the Lord Almighty" (Malachi 3:11 NIV).

In that moment, I asked God about the valuable possessions I had accumulated over time—like stereos, DVD players, and hi-tech kid's games. I questioned God about this scripture. "Lord, does that mean you will prevent thieves from coming and stealing from me?"

That day He did not answer me, but the following day a man looking like a handyman came to my door. He had a tool pouch around his waist and a tape measure in his hand. He said, "Hi! I'm here to measure all your doors and windows in order to fit security screens. Is that okay?"

"Okay," I replied, bewildered. I watched the handyman go about his business. Just as he was about to leave, he spotted the back door between the kitchen and the garage.

"Do you have to do this one too?" I asked.

"Yes, ma'am. The whole house needs to be secure."

"Okay," I said, thinking back to the question I had asked God the day before. Was this the answer I had been looking for?

It was clear government housing was fitting all its houses with security screens, but my explanation sounded more realistic!

Miracle after miracle of financial blessing followed my willingness to tithe and give to God what was rightfully His.

When Bianca came the following day, offering Mack a cleaning position where she worked, we were blessed with a weekly wage and the job was only a hundred meters up the road, easy walking distance.

God's presence was so strong in my life that I could almost see Him. In fact, I could see Him—but not with natural eyes. He was smiling, delighting in me and I basked in the revelation of His love.

Then the Lord began to move in my life in ways I could not explain.

The year 2005 came with many surprises, and with the government handing out cash bonuses, I saw it as nothing short of a financial blessing from God. We had more than enough money to buy our first car, but we had a slight issue—Mack and I were not licensed to drive. We had committed thousands of traffic offences in the other state, accumulating thousands of dollars in fines and suspensions to last a lifetime, and my fines alone were a staggering $9,000. At this stage, the western state didn't have a payment system like the eastern state where we were living. With their payment system, offenders were permitted to pay off fines while still being allowed to drive.

After phoning back west and learning we were not able to have our licenses transferred unless the fines were paid in full, Mack took the chance of applying for a new license, knowing it was an offence to do so. He actually succeeded, so I was tempted to do the same. I walked into the transport office and asked to take the learner test. The woman at the counter passed me the forms and asked me if I had a license in any other state. I replied no.

I took the forms away to a chair and began filling them out. As I was answering the questions, I felt the Holy Spirit's gentle conviction that I was lying. I had to make a decision. It was either lie and get a new license, or tell the truth and never have one again. Did I really want it that badly? Yes, to a certain extent I did, but I had already made a conscious decision to follow God and do things His way. In the past, lies had gotten me nowhere fast, and they always led to negative consequences. I had believed the lies that I created, and out of that belief had come more strife. No, I wanted God's blessing to be in it, and I knew there would be none if I lied and got away with it. Now I knew the truth, and the truth was I would not be getting away with anything. God was watching me. He knew what no one else did, and that mattered most to me. Right in that moment, I asked God to make a way out for me, and I believed He would.

I walked back to the counter with my paperwork. The woman, who was typing away vigorously, stopped and took the papers from me.

Before I could even speak, she blurted out, "You already have a license."

I bowed my head in shame. "I'm sorry. Yes I do, and that's why I didn't finish filling it in."

She paused and then peered down at me through her tiny reading glasses. "Consider yourself lucky. This is a legal document, and I could have had you prosecuted for a false statement had you signed it."

I swallowed hard before telling her of my situation—how badly I needed my license and how I was knocked back when I tried to have it transferred from my home state. After I finished explaining, she relaxed a little and then insisted I phone again. I did not know what good that was going to do, but she said I should try again and explain how much I really needed it.

"All the best with that," she said, and with that I left.

When I got home, I took her advice and gave it another go. To my surprise, the woman who answered the phone advised me that in three months, their transport centre was launching a similar payment system.

"Wow! Three months? Fantastic!" I said.

This was a shorter period than that of waiting to get my license all over again. This news excited me. They had not mentioned any of this when I first rang them. It was as if God had just blessed me for choosing not to commit an offence. For the first time ever

I felt rewarded with a clear conscience. I had nothing to hide, and knowing this brought peace and joy to my soul.

Now the hunt was on to find a family car. Having five children meant we were going to need a bus. Friends from church offered to take us in to the city to look for a vehicle. After driving around the city for most of a day, we came across a bright yellow Mitsubishi Express, and eight-seater van with colourful curtains all around. The price was $1,500, and without even taking it for a spin, we bought it. We were fully aware that it was unregistered and unlicensed, but I drove it home anyway.

We saw many cop cars along the way and hoped and prayed we would not be caught. The van ran pretty well considering it was fourteen years old and had towed a caravan all over Australia. We made it home safely after a three-and-a-half-hour drive, but I felt deeply convicted, for I had intentionally broken the law by driving the van.

If I was determined to live a happy and prosperous life, full of God's blessings, I had to learn to follow the law or I would end up back in the same mess, crying out, "Why, oh why?"

However, I had a major problem with obeying the law.

In the past, I had never trusted anyone, especially cops. I had developed a hatred of such authority, and this was why I found it difficult to obey. My thoughts were always, *Why should I? Some of them are getting away with crimes worse than the ones I'm committing.*

After things I'd experienced, seen, and heard, I had come to hate cops and all they stood for. To me, dirty cops were everywhere. When I was a street kid, some cops would stop to pick up soliciting prostitutes at Bunji Park, and they weren't picking the girls up to arrest them! Then there was the matter of Snake. I'd concluded the reason he had not been interrogated was that he was being protected, and protected by dirty cops. The list went on.

However, as I was focusing on all the reasons that justified my law-breaking, God spoke to me very clearly through my daily reading of His Word, which had become the most important part of my day.

"Let everyone be subject to the governing authorities, for there is no authority except that which God has established. The authorities that exist have been established by God. Consequently, whoever rebels against the authority is rebelling against what God has instituted, and those who do so will bring judgment on themselves" (Romans 13:1–2 NIV).

I heard the Lord say, "When you rebel against them, you rebel against me."

"But Lord, what about their corrupt ways? How can I submit to them?" I argued.

He answered me again through the third verse of the same chapter of Romans. "For rulers hold no terror for those who do right, but for those who do wrong. Do you want to be free from fear of the one in authority? Then do what is right and you will be commended" (Romans 13:3 NIV).

Wow! How powerful, personal, and relevant this scripture was. I had just received a powerful revelation that was going to change me forever and for the better.

My choice to submit was to affect every area of my life, and it started with the way I approached the cops. Never in a million years did I think I would say, "Good day, officers," with a huge smile on my face, but I did. After all, I loved the Lord so much now that whatever He said, I wanted to do. I wanted to please Him even though He was already pleased with me, regardless.

In the quiet and still moments of my life, I often sensed God stirring me with a desire to write. Writing came easy to me in the form of journaling. I loved journaling as a way to express my thoughts and prayers.

One day, while I was having coffee and talking to a friend about my past life as a junkie, I felt God interrupt me. He clearly said, "You're going to write a book about it one day."

When I heard this, I just laughed it off, right in the face of my friend, who probably wondered why I was laughing for no reason. Writing was one of my favourite pastimes, but never in a million years had I dreamed of writing a book.

After hearing from God, I never really gave it much more thought until God started to prod me in the spirit, encouraging me with two words: "The book."

This went on until I realized God was serious, and "the book" was His will for my life—along with being a good wife to my husband and a good mother to my children.

A year had passed by and Mack and I were regularly hosting a life group meeting once a week in the comfort of our own home. Our assistant pastor (a really great guy) led the meetings. As well as being the assistant pastor of our church and leader of our life group, he was also a very good friend, as was his wife, who was our youth leader at the time.

These two wonderful people brought a whole new meaning to friendship. They were very encouraging and supportive of our newly found walk with God. Mack found a good friend in our assistant pastor, and the two of them often went motorbike riding. His wife was like a rare jewel that you find and treasure—a very dear friend. She would often visit, bringing encouragement to Baron, Steele, and Carina, who were attending her youth group.

At last, the kids were living normal stable lives compared to a year ago and God was in the process of building positive relationships for our family, as well as restoring our lives back to good health.

It was at this time that I felt the gentle nudge of conviction, which prompted me to say good-bye to my lifelong trusty friend, nicotine. Nicotine had always been there in times of trouble in the past, but now it was time for us to part ways. I knew it was not going to be easy, so I sought God's counsel. One of His many names refers to Him as being a Counsellor. I found these scriptures while I was reading my Bible one morning.

"For to us a child is born, to us a son is given, and the government will be on his shoulders. And he will be called Wonderful Counsellor, Mighty God, Everlasting Father, Prince of Peace" (Isaiah 9:6 NIV)

Until then I had experienced God's counsel but not actually *read* about it. I was very excited as I read these verses. They described what God had been doing over the years—counselling and leading me out of my life of addiction.

When I sought God's help concerning my smoking, he gave me a strategy to conquer it, through helpful quit smoking tracts.

First I stopped smoking in the house. Then, a few weeks later, I began to delay the favourite morning and after-dinner smokes. Next, I set a date to give up completely in two weeks. As that time drew closer, I asked God for strength and willpower.

One day, as I was sitting on my front porch having a coffee and a smoke, a proud spirit rose up in me. I began imagining how good I would look after I stopped smoking. Suddenly I heard the Lord.

"Do you think you're going to look good when you give up those smokes?"

Puzzled, I listened closely as He continued. "*There's stuff inside you that's worse than that cigarette!*"

It was so profound, I thought I was tripping. "If that's the case, Lord, let's get rid of this habit so we can start on the inner stuff," I replied.

God was right in what He had said. He wasn't looking on the outside. He was more interested in my heart's condition. I had all sorts of issues going on in there. Issues like pride, anger, bitterness, self-pity, greed—you name it, I had it.

I saw that "righteousness" had nothing to do with not smoking or right living. The Bible says we are only made righteous when we look to the Saviour, whose righteous blood covers our *un*righteousness. We are in right standing with God the Father when we *believe* what His Son, Jesus Christ, did on the cross for us.

"This righteousness is given through faith in Jesus Christ to all who believe" (Romans 3:22 NIV).

This revelation set me free. My understanding of wickedness had always been based on people's actual *evil* behaviour. The Word of God was saying that a murderer can be saved if he sincerely repents and believes in the sacrifice of Jesus, who was nailed to the cross to cleanse him of that sin! The word wicked in the Bible is referring to those who have turned away or rejected the sacrifice of God's Son, our Lord and Saviour, Jesus Christ, because they think they can save themselves.

When God said the smoking was nothing compared to my inner condition, I asked Him to begin surgery on my heart, because suddenly I could clearly see, as in a mirror, what was truly going on inside me.

I had thought righteousness was all about "doing good" (external acts), and I was missing the fact that I could never be good because my thoughts alone were evil.

"Everyone has turned away, all have become corrupt; there is no one who does good, not even one" (Psalm 53:3 NIV).

The only one who could save me from myself and cleanse me from all my evil ways was Jesus Christ, God's Son, and I had received His righteousness through faith in Him.

The date I chose to quit smoking was September 22, 2004. Of all the addictions, I found smoking the most difficult one to give up. I really struggled with it. By the second day, my stress levels were low, but I was still badly craving a smoke. The special nicotine gum was making me dizzy, and by the third day, I was ready to quit quitting. However, in that moment, I heard God say, "Let me be your Nicorette."

He wanted me to depend totally on Him, but my body was screaming out for nicotine, and I did not know how to leave it to Him.

As I reached for my smokes, a vision suddenly appeared. Jesus stood between the smokes and me. In a quiet voice, He said, "You couldn't have one even if you wanted to. I have a great plan for your life, and it doesn't involve these."

Dumbfounded, I stared as the vision disappeared. Opening my Bible, I found a verse that confirmed what God had just said. "For I know the plans I have for you," declares the LORD, "plans to prosper you and not to harm you, plans to give you hope and a future" (Jeremiah 29:11 NIV).

Then I saw, as clearly as a big red stop sign, that I wasn't giving up smoking because it's what a Christian *ought* to do—I was giving up *so I could live to do what God had called me to do.*

By this stage I was fighting for my right to live, and I had to really lean on God for strength. Every five minutes I would hear a nagging voice in my head telling me to go outside for a smoke. The nagging would go on all day, even when I occupied myself with more and more tasks around the house. I finally yelled out to God, asking Him to make a way out for me. His answer was for me to go outside when I was tempted and draw in three very deep, slow breaths. Doing this tricked my mind into thinking I was smoking.

I have to confess, it did stop the nagging for a while, but the basic desire to smoke was still there. However, after having the vision and hearing from God, I was determined to keep on fighting. Jesus had spoken to me concerning my future, and that kept me focused on winning. I was committed to overcoming the disgusting habit that had in itself the power to kill.

CHAPTER SIXTEEN

Beauty for Ashes

It was 2005 when I believed God was calling Mack and me to enter into a marriage covenant, a covenant blessed by God and full of blessing. We had been together for eleven years.

When I was very young, I often dreamed about my wedding day, as all little girls do. Years of drug addiction had shattered those dreams, making my future appear only dark and grim. It was after the announcement of Blue and Bianca's wedding that I started to dream again.

Thanks to God, our senior pastor, and his wife, the wedding became a reality. Through the many contributing hands of my wonderful church family, our wedding day was made possible and memorable.

Help started with a $3,000 wedding dress, handed down to me by my beautiful sister Alessia. We also had a professional photographer who took all the photos at no cost. He did this as a gift and a blessing. The wedding cake was professionally made—three layers high with a lit-up pink waterfall underneath. This beautiful wedding cake was also a gift. The wedding car was a borrowed green GTS Monaro with black pinstripes up both sides.

Our reception was in the auditorium of our home church, which overlooks a beautiful creek. The reception came courtesy of our church family, who voluntarily took on the task of catering and decorating. We had a place for our wedding photos near the church, under the beautiful weeping willow trees that swayed softly in the spring air.

However, the most important part of the day was the moment when Mack and I were joined together in a holy covenant with God.

Mack and I had come so far together, and this special day was a symbol of our love for each other. For the first time, I felt my life moving in an upward direction, with God's blessings resting firmly on both our lives. It was truly a perfect day and more than I had ever dreamed it could be.

"The book!"

It was happening again! God was prodding me, reminding me of the book He had said I would someday write.

I questioned Him once more. "Lord, how? I can't write. My English sucks, and my spelling is even worse. I wouldn't know how to start it or even how to go about it."

He reminded me of the many years of journaling I had done and said, "Just get yourself an exercise book and write it like it is from start to finish. Write on the right-hand side of every page and leave the left-hand side blank. That way you can go back and add things you missed."

I blinked, realizing the Lord was serious. He was personally guiding and directing me. My response was to obey Him.

I started thinking about the book day and night until I was dreaming about it. I had so many questions about the whole issue. They all began with, "How?"

I prayed, "How will I type it out and get it published?" As clear as day, He said, "Just start writing, and I will do the rest."

So I did! I bought an exercise book, just like the Lord had said, and just in case one of my kids found it and decided to have a scribble in it, I wrote on the cover with a black Nikon pen, "DO NOT TOUCH—MY BOOK 1."

However, I still didn't know how to start it.

A week went by and nothing. It was just sitting there.

Occasionally I would look over at the book as I went about my daily chores, and I would pray, asking God to help me. Then, on September 16 I woke up, and as I lay there half-awake, half-asleep, a voice in my head read out what sounded like a page from my past. The words etched themselves in my mind so deeply that I did not need to record them. *Not once did I ever see my father loving my mother, or vice versa.*

I sat up! Wow, finally I had something clear to start with.

Every night after the kids went to bed, I spent time with God, recollecting my past and writing it down. There were nights I would get agitated in my efforts to track and retrace events, working from one scenario in my life to the next. After much praying (usually ending up with me sprawled out on the table), it would all come back to me.

Soon after I began, I was in church chatting with the senior pastor's wife. Somehow we got onto the subject of typing, and she began talking about her typing speed. My eyes lit up. That was exactly what I needed—a speed-typist. I began explaining to her that I was writing my life story and was in need of a typist. She happily agreed to do some typing, which made me wonder if this was what God meant when he said that he would "do the rest."

Another sign came the next day when I received a phone call from the very dear woman who had made my wedding cake. Now she was offering me her old computer and printer because she had upgraded to a new one. I did not know what to say. First, I wasn't used to people giving me things, and second, I had never used a computer. It was something I had never intended buying. I sensed God knew and that this computer was being given for the express purpose of finishing my story.

God was equipping me to do what He had asked me to do, in clear and amazing ways. Yet the dream still seemed far out of reach.

At the same time, I was wrestling with the symptoms of hepatitis C, the disease I had contracted twelve years ago. This made the project of writing the book very hard, as I easily got tired and irritable. Some days the whites of my eyes where yellow, a sign that my liver was indeed struggling. I desperately needed a cure.

Ironically, at this time Mack suddenly fell ill with a hepatitis C infection. God was faithful and led him to a specialist in a neighbouring city an hour or so away. After seeing the specialist and having several blood tests, the results showed that Mack had elevated liver functions. He was encouraged to undergo an intense liver treatment.

The doctor explained to Mack that this treatment was very intense and would require a supportive, loving family. He was given a DVD on the subject for the whole family to watch. He also had to be seen by a psychiatrist to make sure he was mentally and emotionally sound, as the treatment had been known to cause suicide from severe depression and other side effects such as flu-type symptoms, fatigue, and a decrease in the white blood count and platelet count. Other effects were depression, irritability, sleep disturbance, anxiety, and personality changes. This was not going to be an easy process!

We were told that all of the above could be managed but that counselling was going to be necessary throughout. The doctor described the treatment as "mild chemotherapy." Neither of us would truly know what we were in for until we actually started it.

Mack had to be on the treatment for forty-eight weeks—approximately eleven months. He started treatment on November 19, 2005, just under one month after we were married. Mack had to travel to his appointments every month and was required to take three particular tablets twice a day, combined with a weekly injection of powerful drugs, administered in and around the stomach and thigh area. After three months, he responded to the treatment, which was a good sign that it was working.

After receiving such good news, Mack suggested I should do the treatment as well, once he was finished. I was not keen on all the travelling. I said if the clinic moved to where we were living, I would think about it.

Four months into the treatment, I noticed Mack looking rather vacant and showing signs of anxiety and depression. He was emotional about stuff that would never have bothered him before, and he was restless at night. In spite of the many challenges, Mack kept going, and after picking up a contract job cleaning, he came up with an idea to start his own cleaning business in the caravan park where he had been working.

Mack registered his business, and I believe God blessed this venture when some dear church friends invited us over for dinner and gave us much-appreciated advice on business management. They had a business of their own and gave us $2,000, a kick-start toward the cost of buying much-needed equipment. They prayed over us, asking God to bless our business, declaring that we were fertile grounds for the sowing of the $2,000 seed. These two people brought joy and encouragement to our lives. We love these people.

While Mack was going through the treatment, he received some bad news. His mother had an aneurism in her brain and had to have surgery to correct it. This played on all our minds, especially Mack's. As if that was not enough, his father was not well either. In March 2006, Mack's mum underwent surgery on her aneurism, which left her handicapped and unable to look after herself. Thankfully, her new husband was supportive and cared for her needs at the time. This came as a relief to the entire family.

Toward the end of Mack's treatment, one of the side effects was insomnia, and Mack was up at all hours of the night. This was frustrating, as it also affected my sleep. When the medication to help him sleep was not strong enough, he went back to smoking marijuana again after being drug-free for almost four years. This backtracking devastated me. I felt I had no control over his decision to use it again.

Finally, Mack ended his treatment, two weeks shy of the eleven-month course, complaining that he could not take it anymore; he felt like he was going mad. However, six months later Mack was triumphant when his first test for the virus came back negative and the treatment was declared a success.

Days after this good news, Mack's support nurse called and advised that a clinic was opening in our area. She asked if I was keen to undergo the same treatment.

One week later, I was having a scan on my liver as well as blood tests. I was ready to start the treatment. I knew God could supernaturally heal me, but I felt taking the treatment was the way He wanted me to go.

My test results confirmed that like Mack, I had the genotype 1 strain, the hardest strain of hepatitis C to treat. Eleven long months of treatment were ahead of me. That day they handed me my treatment pack, which contained instructions, a weekly pillbox, a chill bag to keep the injections cool, and a diary to record my progress.

The date was 27th July 2007.

Day one! Friday was my chosen injection day, as this would give me a couple of days to get over the peak reaction to it. By Monday I would be able to get the kids off to school.

Some of the symptoms I experienced after my first injection were headaches, a rash that appeared on my ankle, shortness of breath, tiredness, and mood swings. I was already feeling the effects and wondered how I was going to cope if this got worse.

Three months later, and my first blood tests showed I was responding to the treatment. (At this stage, if there is no response, patients are taken off the treatment.) This encouraged me to go on, but it was getting harder.

I have never been one to suffer overly much with depression, but on this particular day, the depression was heavy. In times like this, I would usually find comfort in reading my Bible, but strangely, I could not even comprehend what I was reading. I would go back again and try to absorb it, but nothing. I tried writing and found I could not even do that.

Before the treatment I was into fitness and would exercise daily, but now I was experiencing aches and continuous pain in my calves and ankles. I cannot tell you how frustrated I felt. I was convinced I was losing control of my life, unable to do the things I enjoyed. This depressed me even more. I had a busy lifestyle and needed my health if I was going to get the work done.

Each new day I would desperately draw nearer to God, where I would find new strength to go on.

CHAPTER SEVENTEEN

True Blue

Two months later, Blue was found lying by the front door of his house, conscious but not responding. He was rushed to hospital by ambulance with a suspected drug overdose.

Blue had a history of drug use, which was known by the staff at the local hospital, where he went to get his clean needles. The doctors automatically assumed it was drug-related and said whatever he had taken should wear off soon.

Mack and Ziggy nursed Blue all night, staying with him in the hospital, but there was no change in his condition. The next morning it was realized that there was a far more serious issue going on. He was immediately flown to another major hospital, where they were able to do more for him. We nervously waited to hear from the hospital as we made our way there. They finally phoned and told us to expect the worst.

On arrival, the nurses took us into a room, informing us that Blue had suffered two massive brain haemorrhages. We were told nothing more could be done for him. Blue was heavily sedated and on life support. We needed to make a decision about turning off the machine.

This was to be the saddest and most tragic day of my entire life. My heart went out to his family, especially Mack, who was completely distraught. He had already gone through the trauma of seeing his mother disabled, and now his little brother was at the point of death. The awful decision was going to affect every area of his life, especially his newfound faith in God, which in that moment was being tested to the very core.

The nurse encouraged Mack to say good-bye, and we all gathered round Blue's bed. Grief and sorrow filled the room. I took Blue's hand and held it for the last time, hoping there might still be time for a miracle and wishing it was not good-bye.

After some time, Mack nodded and gave the go-ahead. They switched off the machines and each of our children sobbed. "Good-bye, Uncle Blue; we're gonna miss you." Then, with the last beat of his heart, he was gone.

Blue died on September 17, 2007, following a shot of methyl amphetamines. He suffered a major brain bleed and died the next day. He was only twenty-nine. We were left with the realization that our lives without him would never be the same.

Losing Blue was a terrible tragedy. Life was already hard enough. Now, with the loss of our little brother, things just seemed too much. Going by the phone calls my parents received from me, my parents felt compelled to come over and lend a helping hand.

I was halfway through the treatment and had noticed my sleep patterns changing. I would go to bed exhausted but could not sleep a wink through the night. During the day I felt disoriented from the insomnia. I phoned the hepatitis C nurse, and she suggested I get some sleeping medication.

I had not taken any drugs for four years and did not intend to start again. Sleep medication can be highly addictive, and I just didn't want to have to cope with that on top of the treatment medication.

As I was refusing her suggestion, she said bluntly, "You can't fight this one. You'll just have to put everything off for another seven months, and hang on for the ride."

After she put it like that, I went to see a doctor and he prescribed a nerve relaxant. However, I took less than the prescribed dose as I did not want to get hooked.

One morning I woke up unable to breathe properly. I went to wash my face with cold water. Looking in the mirror, I saw that my face was puffy and my mind felt like mush. I became hysterical, crying to Mack that I did not feel well. He suggested we go to the hospital. Just as he was getting the car ready, the phone rang and it was the hepatitis C nurse. I was surprised that she had phoned, asking me how I was feeling. Did she have ESP?

"No, I'm not doing well. I'm about to go to hospital," I cried.

She explained, "I have your last blood test results in front of me. It shows your haemoglobin count is low and your thyroid has stopped working."

She explained how the thyroid is a gland that makes and stores hormones; hormones help regulate our heart rate, blood pressure, body temperature, and other important functions. My thyroid gland had stopped working. She also told me that I had anaemia (a low number of red blood cells in the blood), which was causing shortness of breath.

Oh my gosh! No wonder I felt so sick.

The nurse suggested I drop one of the doses of the treatment to help with the anaemia and go straight to the hospital to get treatment for the thyroid. The doctor at the hospital put me on thyroid hormone-replacement medication, and with the first dose, I instantly felt better. I still had five months of treatment remaining and could not wait for it all to be over.

As I got closer to the end, I started to lose touch with reality and noticed I was not myself anymore. My relationships were suffering, and everyone around me was in the line of fire. I was emotionally attacking some of my dearest friends from church, and there were days I didn't even want to go to the shops because I felt afraid of people. Some kind of paranoia was tormenting me, and I knew what Mack had been talking about when he said he thought he was going mad.

I also felt distant from God, as though there was a wall between us. I felt less sensitive to His Spirit, which bothered me a lot, but I hung in there with lots of prayer. I believe my church family were also praying.

Finally, the long-awaited day came, and on July 27, 2008, I had my last injection. I was so relieved that the treatment was finally over, but it took another six months before I started to feel better.

After the treatment was finished, I waited anxiously for the results of my blood tests—which came back negative. The hepatitis C was gone! The treatment had been successful as we had hoped and prayed it would be, all praise and thanks to God!

With my healing complete, I looked forward to getting back to the things I was doing before I began the treatment. Even more important, I felt a prompting in my spirit to resume writing my story.

I recommenced writing in July 2009, a year after I had finished the hepatitis C treatment.

At this time, God opened a door of opportunity for me to study certificate IV in theology through Bible college. It was an external course and completed in the comfort of our own church. It was something I had wanted to do for a long time, but due to my very important calling as a mother when my children were still in need of my immediate care, it had not been possible.

Even though God was doing a mighty work in my life, our household was falling apart. My eldest son, Baron, who had completed a five-year traineeship as a boner and slicer at the local meatworks, was drowning in alcoholism and drug addiction. My other son, Steele, who was also striving to complete a traineeship in horticulture, was a little wiser when it came to harder drugs but was also heavily addicted to marijuana. Finally, Carina, who was only thirteen, was smoking more marijuana than both of them put together.

For many years, Mack's family used marijuana extensively. Mack's mother had been introduced to it in her late twenties and had smoked it ever since. Her children grew up thinking this was normal. Ziggy had started smoking when he was eleven, stealing it from his mum's boyfriend. Mack was fourteen when his mum first found out he was smoking, and Blue was caught rolling a joint in his room when he was just nine. Smoking dope had become a pattern that started early in the morning around the kitchen table and ended at bedtime. One generation later, my children were growing up to do just the same. The environment had not changed due to Mack and Ziggy's heavy use of cannabis.

I had such high expectations for my children in spite of where they had come from, and it angered me to see history repeating itself. I was constantly on their case about their drug issues, trying to change the situation. Finally, when that was not helping, I cried out to God, and the Holy Spirit counselled me with his words of wisdom. "You cannot have such high expectations after what they have seen in their lives. They need unconditional love and acceptance, just as I have loved and accepted you."

"Wow! You're right, Lord. But how do I do it?" I asked.

I needed to make a concerted effort to stop being critical and angry, as this was how they were perceiving God. God wanted me to support, encourage, and love them—with the same unconditional love He had given me.

I was going to need His help in this because His way was the opposite of mine. In my quest for His help, I began to search my Bible for answers on the subject, to see what God's views were. After all, He is the Master of unconditional love.

I found an answer in Romans 5:8: "But God demonstrates his own love for us in this: While we were still sinners, Christ died for us" (NIV).

I could not get any more "unconditional" than that, could I?

I made it my goal to try to change my perspective and love my family unconditionally.

I felt alone in my walk with God even though I was surrounded by family. I took things one day at a time. My husband was sinking deeper and deeper into depression over the loss of his brother and his mother's medical condition. He was relying more and more on drugs, rather than on God. I felt as though we were drifting apart. Then I read 2 Corinthians 12:9 (NIV): "My grace is sufficient for you, for my power is made perfect in weakness. Therefore I will boast all the more gladly about my weaknesses, so that Christ's power may rest on me."

Living around a husband and children who were in bondage to drug addiction was very difficult. I wanted my home to be a place of refuge and free from addictions, not the other way round. When God told me I should love them and support them rather than rouse on them, I found it very difficult to obey. After all, I was my children's mother and wanted to set an example now that I was clean.

I realized my home had a smoking room (also known as a laundry), and my husband was spending more time out there smoking than in the house with us. If I wanted to communicate with my husband and three older children, the laundry was where I would have to go.

I was constantly throwing tantrums over the marijuana being smoked in our home, and I repeatedly threatened to kick Mack out. This only upset our two daughters, Storm and Sky, who would start hitting me and crying, "Leave our dad alone." It was as if I was the one in the wrong.

I blamed my husband for my children's addictions, and he replied by saying that he worked hard and was entitled to smoke it "as a recreational time-waster." To me it sounded like he was saying, "I don't care!" I would run into my room, slam the door in frustration, and cry, lying on the floor. I did not want to be in that environment. I wanted out.

I had suffered drug addiction for most of my life, and I did not want it around me anymore. I was so very aware of God's rich promises and thought Mack's bad choices would prevent me from receiving them. I even asked the Lord to separate us if it was not His will for us to be together, but nothing happened, so I saw this as a sign to keep going and stay put.

One morning, as I was wrestling with God in prayer about Mack's drug problem, I had a sudden revelation that brought a lot of peace into my life. It was through my Bible reading that I received this truth, and it blew me away. "For the unbelieving husband has been sanctified through his wife" (1 Corinthians 7 v 14 NIV).

I ran for the phone and rang our pastor while Mack was in the laundry. Whispering, I asked him what the scripture meant. I wanted to know if God's blessings on my own life could be affected by anything Mack did, no matter what it was. I also wanted to know if it was saying that Mack was "sanctified" through *my* faith in Christ Jesus. (Sanctified means purified from sin.) My pastor responded with a clear yes.

I was so excited that I jumped for joy. This revelation did not eliminate the drug problem, but it calmed the spiritual battle within me. I had thought I would have to suffer the consequences of *Mack's* bad choices. Now that I had this scripture, I felt free and stopped harassing him—for a little while anyway.

In the middle of all this, and in spite of Mack's habits, God was calling me to respect my husband, which challenged me to trust God on a higher level. "You want me to do what, Lord?"

"Give him what he wants," the Lord said.

Mack often asked me for money to buy more weed after he had run out. He was smoking $50 worth a day, and that was on a good day. I struggled with his request because firstly, I did not think he should be smoking, and secondly, I was living on a budget. I did not want to give him our last $50 to buy pot so he could get smashed and not care about anything.

"Sounds pretty selfish to me," I reasoned. However, I knew what it was like to be addicted to drugs—it seems as though the whole world revolves around it and nothing else matters. I felt angry and jealous, as I wanted Mack to be into *me*, to give *me* all that attention. Then God reminded me of a time when I was the same.

No matter how *right* I felt in the middle of this particular battle, I heard God's voice saying, "Give him what he wants."

I often went walking around five in the morning. One particular morning I left the house in a rage of anger. Mack and I had been arguing about him wanting a $50 bag again so soon. I recalled that the Holy Spirit had told me to give Mack what he wanted. Struggling with this, I walked, prayed, and tried to justify my unwillingness to obey God. The more I blamed Mack, the more I felt convicted that *I* was disobeying God. I knew I was in the wrong. With fists clenched and my face screwed up, I would power-walk to get rid of the frustrations.

I cried, "Why, Lord? Why do I have to give him what he wants? It's not fair. This is all the money I have left. Why should I give him what he wants?"

I kept walking as I waited to hear back from God. Then, out of the corner of my eye, I spotted a crisp, clean $50 note lying in the gutter. It was as though God had dropped it fresh out of heaven. I heard God's voice clearly say "Trust me and give him what he wants."

His words rang through my entire body like a giant gong! He had just shown me how simply and easily He could provide. I was truly blown away, and it made me realize I was not struggling with Mack but with God.

Mack wasn't the problem—I was!

I had to question how much I really trusted God, and the answer was—not much!

I was disappointed Mack had relapsed into his old habits, but we had married with a clean start, and I wanted our marriage to work. That's when God led me to read about marriage and order in the family. "Wives, submit yourselves to your own husbands as you do to the Lord. For the husband is the head of the wife as Christ is the head of the church, His body, of which He is the Saviour" (Ephesians 5:22–23 NIV).

Even though I believed I had it more together than everyone else did, God was calling me to put my trust in Him by submitting to my husband, who was making wrong choices.

As I kept reading the scriptures, I found verses for husbands telling them to respect and honour their wives and stuff like that. I roused on God, telling Him my husband was not doing any of those things. In fact, he was doing worse now than before we got married.

The Lord promised me that if I would just do my part, He would deal with the husband parts Himself.

First I had to do my part, faithfully and consistently. "Wives, in the same way submit yourselves to your own husbands so that, if any of them do not believe the word, they may be won over without words by the behaviour of their wives" (1 Peter 3:1 NIV).

Suddenly I received revelation of what God was showing me. As much as I wanted my husband to be all God intended him to be, I myself could not change him. Getting upset and throwing tantrums was actually showing that I had little faith and no trust in God.

Struggling with that thought, I made a firm decision. Beginning that day, I would trust God and take Him at His word.

I knew it was not going to be easy. To me, submitting to someone who was off his or her face was the equivalent of jumping off a cliff and wondering if God would actually catch me.

I had days when I was at peace, placing my whole situation in God's hands, but then I would break out and start fighting with the family, trying to kick them out of the house all over again.

It was a vicious cycle, and I always ended up in my room crying to God. As time went by, though, God showed me that the things I disapproved of so much would someday be in the past. He was going to make it all right if I would just be still and put my trust in Him each day. "Be still, and know that I am God" (Psalm 46:10 NIV).

I was desperate to please God. I was trying to please Him in the way I lived, but the truth was my reaction toward my family's behaviour was worse than what they were doing.

That's when I heard the Lord say, "My child, I know you want to live in such a way, but I love these people. I'm not looking at their behaviour. It's okay; my Grace is sufficient for this situation and all you need to do is trust me."

Once again I paid attention, wondering if I was hearing it right. Was the Lord saying this was all okay? Oh my goodness! It was all back to front. Everything I was ever taught about God was all backward. I was raised to believe God would want me to leave my situation, but instead He was insisting I *stay* in it. I could not help but feel angry toward God. I declared that I wanted out, because Storm and Sky were living in an environment I did not want for them.

"Get me out of this place," I cried.

"Okay! You want to go live your little straight life, in your little straight house away from everyone. Then who will you minister to?"

The Holy Spirit had just confronted me concerning His will for my life.

It was right in that moment that I realized my life was exactly how God wanted it. Even though my family was living contrary to His will, He loved them dearly. This was indeed God's perfect *will* for my life, and I needed to abandon *my* wants for what God wanted for them.

Despite the lack of order in the house and the violation of every rule *I* wanted my family to follow, I knew joy—inner joy that came only from the Lord. I began to realize God was changing me in the way I thought and fought about things. I began choosing my battles more wisely because God was giving me visions of hope concerning my children.

He also gave me a vision of my husband, unbelievable as it looked. In the vision, Mack was standing over his Bible at the kitchen table, praying in tongues and waving his fist, declaring the promises of God. As He showed me this, His voice thundered in my spirit: "I can do this; you can't!"

This vision was unreal, for I knew how far from God Mack was. However, it excited me. I *knew* God loved him. God had sanctified him through our marriage, had set him apart for salvation, and I knew only God could bring about the changes I desired for my husband.

CHAPTER EIGHTEEN

Eight Years Later

These days I still struggle in the area of trust, but I am getting better at listening to God and obeying Him, which brings a great deal of peace and joy to my daily life.

My three eldest children, Baron, Steele, and Carina, are still finding their way. I continue to believe each one of them will grow in their faith and be awesome members of God's family.

The truth is we will not see perfection in our lives until Jesus returns, and this gives me great peace, knowing God has it all under control.

My desire is that all my children grow up to honour God with all their heart and soul, and live lives for his Son, Jesus.

I don't care much for higher education, although it is good in itself. To be educated in the things of God and His kingdom ranks first with me, for these things have eternal value.

Our two little girls, Storm and Sky, are growing up fast. They have both been planted firmly in the house of God since their birth. Storm, at age twelve, is a mighty prayer warrior and already has great faith. Although she was born with a heroin addiction, she is a very healthy and bright young girl with a very strong character. I thank God for her health and strength. Sky is a wonderful young lady and also doing well. God had assured me both girls would be fine and they are. God is good.

My husband, Mack, has made the decision to follow Jesus, and I look forward to seeing that vision of my husband worshiping and living for God realized. God knows that together, Mack and I can both do great things for His glory.

Mack's brother, Ziggy, is still very much a part of our family as he is the father of Baron, Steele, and Carina. He recently made a commitment to know Christ Jesus and attends church regularly. I believe the sky is the limit for him in achieving his goals.

CHAPTER NINETEEN

Scars into Stars

When God told me to write my story, I personally did not feel it would be of interest to anyone, but He made it clear He wanted it done.

I have been writing *For This Cause* on and off for eight years, and it has been the focus in my life. The enemy (Satan) has tried hard to discourage me, with tactics that have included voices in my head saying things like, "Pfft, who are you to write a book? You failed at English; you can't write!"

I was distracted by Satan's lie, and for weeks, I would not write. Then God gave me a vision. It was a scene from a movie complete with surround sound. I believe God showed me that this book will be huge and that it will someday become a blockbuster movie.

Yet even though I was surrendered, sold out for Jesus and His cause for my life, the book was a burden because I felt utterly inadequate. Despite these feelings, I encouraged myself.

"If God says it will someday be a movie, it will be!" God also blew me away when He said, "And you will meet Oprah".

Right after hearing this from God, this particular celebrity decided to end her shows. Was this another one of Satan's tricks to have me doubt God at His word? If God says I will meet her, then I will and I believe she needs to meet me.

I was in total awe of what God was showing me, and writing this book became the most important task in my life, along with being a better wife to my husband and mother to my children.

Because the book was important to God, it became very important to me. I found the more I doubted, the more God encouraged me, with visions from what I had already written. The book became a reality right before my eyes.

The events surrounding Snake still haunt me, and to this day it remains a mystery. However, I do know that after my phone call to the hotline, the killings stopped and there have been no more reports, which has made me wonder if God actually used me to put a stop to his crimes.

When I think back to that time I cringe because I know God was protecting me and has done so all the way.

> Whoever dwells in the shelter of the Most High will rest in the shadow of the Almighty.
>
> I will say of the LORD, "He is my refuge and my fortress, my God, in whom I trust."
>
> Surely he will save you from the fowler's snare and from the deadly pestilence.
>
> He will cover you with his feathers, and under his wings you will find refuge; his faithfulness will be your shield and rampart.
>
> You will not fear the terror of night, nor the arrow that flies by day, nor the pestilence that stalks in the darkness, nor the plague that destroys at midday.
>
> A thousand may fall at your side, ten thousand at your right hand, but it will not come near you.
>
> You will only observe with your eyes and see the punishment of the wicked.

If you say, "The LORD is my refuge," and you make the Most High your dwelling, no harm will overtake you, no disaster will come near your tent.

For he will command his angels concerning you to guard you in all your ways; they will lift you up in their hands, so that you will not strike your foot against a stone.

You will tread on the lion and the cobra; you will trample the great lion and the serpent.

"Because he loves me," says the LORD, "I will rescue him; I will protect him, for he acknowledges my name.

"He will call on me, and I will answer him; I will be with him in trouble, I will deliver him and honour him.

"With long life I will satisfy him and show him my salvation." (Psalm 91 NIV)

When I first started writing, I intended to leave the account of what happened with Snake out of the book. However, God loves justice (Isaiah 61:8).

For those women who were brutally killed, I pray they get the justice they deserve. My heart and sincere condolences go out to the victims' families. I pray they will one day get the answers they need to lay their loved ones to rest. After they do, I pray they will allow Jesus to comfort them and fill them with His peace.

As for me, I look forward to the day of the Lord, when all wickedness will be judged. I have hated the world and its system ever since I can remember, and I am waiting for the promise of a new system where Christ reigns among us. There will be no more pain and sorrow, only peace and an everlasting life with our Maker.

It is going to be awesome! "But as it is written: 'Eye has not seen, nor ear heard, nor have entered into the heart of man the things which God has prepared for those who love Him'" (1 Corinthians 2:9 NKJV).

God gave our family stability when He blessed us with our awesome home in this lovely town. We have been living here for ten years now and attending our home church for nine. We have rarely missed a Sunday service except when we have gone on holidays.

Church has been the source of everything I need to fulfil my calling. For example, my book has been written with the aid of Christian brothers and sisters who attend our church and have specific skills.

I believe the book would not have been possible without me being part of God's awesome church. I love all my church family with great affection.

Church is everything, and I feel a strong connection to it. It is where I meet with the family of God, and together we *are* the church.

The Bible calls the church the body of Christ, of which Christ is the head. Together we are His body on the earth, executing justice and goodwill toward all people from every walk of life.

Following is a poem titled "The Church of the Lord Jesus Christ." It is an ode to the beautiful "Body of Christ, the Church," and is reproduced here with the kind permission of the author, Richard Fergusson.

> "She is the plan of God on earth; always in her Father's eye: cherished, mysterious, beautiful, and potent beyond measure, King-empowered and life-infused. She emerges triumphant; limitless with potential; a harbour for the hopeless and an answer

for the ages: the church resplendent—a bride for His Son.

She is the body of Christ on earth; born, like her Head, amidst tribulation, under jealous skies. Cradled in her innocence and guarded for His purpose. She grows in wisdom and stature with victory on her lips and freedom in her hands. Hers is an unstoppable cause. She embraces the world with dignity, honour, and compassion; gives vision to the sightless and life to the dying.

She is the family of God on earth. Within her compass, the hungry find sustenance and the weary receive strength. She is a haven for recovering humanity, enthralled by grace. She invites the broken, the vulnerable, and the outcast to be immersed in love. She stands imperfect but perfection resides within her. She is flawed but is washed with forgiveness. She has a treasury of faith and a wealth of belonging.

She is the house of heaven on earth: a representative, resolute to reconcile. The Word within her accepts the receptive but challenges the heartless. She is the ecclesia, called out to serve the world: calling out to welcome in. Blood-washed and armed with testimony, the cross on her lips liberates the chained and offends the unchanging. Like her Master, she is pursued and persecuted. Yet she rises with strength in her heart and fire in her soul.

She is the bride of Christ on earth; readying herself for the day when all eyes will be upon her. Prepared and presented before the Lord: The Lamb for whom the world waits, who comes like the rising sun, majestic and magnificent beyond description, while she dazzles with reflected glory. Spotless,

perfect and mature, she bows low to cast her crowns
and passionately worship Him. Her temporal focus
becomes her eternal gaze. She is the church of the
Lord Jesus Christ."

Going by what this poem says, I am part of something really big.
God is using His church to bring about His purpose and kingdom
on earth, and I am so excited to be part of it.

God's plan for the church is to bring salvation to a dying world by
commanding/commissioning us to go preach (share) the Gospel (the
good news of salvation) to everyone.

The Great Commission of Jesus Christ is: "Therefore go and
make disciples of all nations, baptizing them in the name of the
Father and of the Son and of the Holy Spirit, and teaching them to
obey everything I have commanded you. And surely I am with you
always, to the very end of the age" (Matthew 28:19–20 NIV).

We are messengers! God has given us the privilege of spreading
the good news of His love and gift of salvation to others. He does
not want anyone to suffer eternity without His love and presence, so
He uses us, His Church (His people) to share the wonderful message
of hope. This is called evangelism. As Christians, it is vital to pass
on God's message of love and hope and never stop praying daily for
those who are still unsaved.

"The Lord is not slow in keeping his promise, as some understand
slowness. Instead he is patient with you, not wanting anyone to
perish, but everyone to come to repentance" (2 Peter 3:9 NIV).

I have recently completed my certificate IV in theology (Bible
college), and I believe it was part of God's plan for me. It has been
a great aid in the writing of my story. Even more importantly, it has
taught me a great deal about God the Father, His Beloved Son, Jesus,

and their awesome loving plan to save humanity from the curse of sin and death.

The good news of Jesus Christ is found in John 3:16: "For God so loved the world that he gave his one and only Son, that whoever believes in him shall not perish but have eternal life" (NIV).

Wow! Now I understand fully the words God thundered to me—that I was "*never* going to die." He was talking about eternal life—life beyond the grave—the *free gift* I received when I first believed and committed my life to my Saviour, *Jesus*! This incredible gift cannot be earned by doing good things; it is free to whomever believes.

I am so grateful for what Jesus did that I want to tell the world about it. I now enjoy my own personal ministry of reaching out to my community and shining the light of Christ—by loving God, loving people, and loving life.

Jesus is my all in all; whatever I need, He is. More than anything, I desire His awesome presence in my life.

The Bible is my roadmap, my compass for living. It helps me stay on track, as I do not ever want to get lost in the wilderness of life again.

I am on a journey, desiring to become more and more like my Saviour, Jesus Christ, who is the Author and Finisher of my faith. Even though I stuff up daily, the blood of Jesus cleanses me. I am filled and overflowing with joy knowing God has my life and the lives of my husband and children covered.

I am constantly learning to trust God in all circumstances. "If we confess our sins, he is faithful and just and will forgive us our sins and purify us from all unrighteousness" (1 John 1:9 NIV).

Hallelujah! How liberating is that? I am free to be me. "Then you will know the truth, and the truth will set you free" (John 8:32 NIV).

When I finally met with Jesus (God's *living* word) and committed my life to His "cause," I found an instant purpose to live. Without that purpose I would have died a junkie, for life itself hadn't had anything to offer me.

I have learnt that faith in God requires I read my Bible daily, as it is important for my spiritual growth. The Bible is regarded as God's Word, and every word in it is food for my soul. Without it, I would die a spiritual death.

"Jesus answered, 'It is written: "Man shall not live on bread alone, but on every word that comes from the mouth of God"'" (Mathew 4:4 NIV).

I also noticed that it was not until I started reading the Bible and applying it to my life that I was able to overcome my battles. Believing in God was simply not enough. Our pastor once used a phrase when he taught in a religious instruction class at the local high school: "It's not what you know but *who* you know." I was lacking the *true* knowledge of God, which can only come from reading what the Bible says about Him. "My people are destroyed from lack of knowledge" (Hosea 4:6 NIV).

God's Word is described as being alive and active. It has proven to be powerful once applied, in that it has guided me through everyday life, giving an answer to every problem, and challenging me to be the best I can be. "For the word of God is alive and active. Sharper than any double-edged sword, it penetrates even to dividing soul and spirit, joints and marrow; it judges the thoughts and attitudes of the heart" (Hebrews 4:12 NIV).

Reading daily from my Bible has been a crucial part of my recovery. I am proud to say I have been clean (drug free) for ten years.

I am really excited about the future. The Bible says God has an awesome plan for me, and even though I wasted twenty-five years of my life, the best is yet to come!

"For I know the plans I have for you," declares the Lord, "plans to prosper you and not to harm you, plans to give you hope and a future" (Jeremiah 29:11 NIV).

God's passion to save humanity has become my mission. If I can bring hope to just one person, then it has been well worth it, and I will have fulfilled that purpose.

His love and kindness have turned my test into a testimony, and my scars into stars. Through every bad and sinful situation, God covered me with His grace. He alone gave me great strength and courage to endure it all, so that now my story—His story—can be shared; not for fame but to benefit others.

"You (Satan) intended to harm me, but God intended it for good to accomplish what is now being done, the saving of many lives" (Genesis 50:20 NIV).

CHAPTER TWENTY

Making You Famous Jesus

God has saved me from a life of destruction and given me a mission. He has commissioned me to take my story and the gospel (truth about Jesus, who He is, what He has done for everyone and me) to the ends of the earth. I am focused and running with this truth as if I were running for gold, passing on the baton of the Great Commission to the next generation in the grand race that the Bible calls "the race of faith."

> Therefore we also, since we are surrounded by so great a cloud of witnesses, let us lay aside every weight, and the sin which so easily ensnares us, and let us run with endurance the race that is set before us, looking unto Jesus, the author and finisher of our faith, who for the joy that was set before Him endured the cross, despising the shame, and has sat down at the right hand of the throne of God. (Hebrews 12:1–2 NKJV)

God's heart and passion to save humanity is now my mission, and nothing else matters to me more. For this cause I was born.

Glory to God!

Amen!

If you declare with your mouth, "Jesus is Lord" and believe in your heart that God raised him from the dead, you will be saved. For it is with your heart that you believe and are justified, and it is with your mouth that you profess your faith and are saved. As Scripture says, "Anyone who believes in him will never be put to shame." For there is no difference between Jew and Gentile—the same Lord is Lord of all and richly blesses all who call on him (Romans 10:9–12 NIV).

A Prayer

"Heavenly Father, I come to You in the name of Jesus, and I confess I have sinned against You. Forgive me. I believe Your Son, Jesus Christ, died on the cross to pay for my sin and rose from the dead on the third day. He is alive today, and I put my faith and trust only in Jesus Christ to forgive and save me from the penalty of my sin. I confess Jesus as my Lord and Saviour, and I receive His precious gift of eternal life. Thank you for loving me; I thank you for it in Jesus's name, amen."

ACKNOWLEDGEMENTS

I would like to thank my Lord God and Saviour first, for the amazing way He has guided me in this huge exercise. He gave me the courage to write my story and kept me going. Thanks to Him I have a new life and know real blessings, great and small, every single day.

I would like to thank our (now retired) senior pastor and his wife for their love and support from day one. Their help and encouragement has been invaluable.

I would also like to express my thanks and appreciation to all who have contributed their time and skills, helping shape this book and prepare it for publication.

I want to give a special enormous thank you to my family. They have been travelling this journey with me. We have been through so much together, and as I have been writing this book, they have been reliving some of the events with me. I love all of my family deeply and appreciate their patience, love, and support through it all. I pray that as they see the new person I am today, by the power of Jesus Christ, they will be encouraged to let God work in and through their own lives in the coming years.

There are many other folk I could list here, who have been friends of our family for many years. They know who they are, and I send them all a grateful thank you.

I would also like to thank Balboa Press for their guidance and assistance throughout the publishing process.

May God bless and be with you all.

ABOUT THE AUTHOR

Nascosta InCristo lives in a rural town in Queensland with her husband and two younger children. Her home has a constant stream of visiting family members and friends. She continues to be a strong, active member in her church and is well known as a positive, vibrant, and faith-filled member of the local community.

Printed in the United States
By Bookmasters